"One does what one must to make a living," Lugosi said. "Dying for me is a living."

They weren't buying it.

We were in the lair of the Dark Knights of Transylvania. Someone had been threatening Bela for more than a month, nasty notes and warnings to "stay away." The topper had been the hat box with the cute little bat in it, a cute little bat with a cute little stake stuck into it.

Lugosi had shrugged it off as a sick prank. I wasn't so sure. And the crowd around us tonight did nothing to restore my confidence.

NEVER CROSS

CROSS

— A —

VAMPIRE

Stuart Kaminsky

First Mysterious Press Edition March, 1984

2 4 6 8 0 9 7 5 3 1

Library of Congress Catalogue Number: 83-63281
    ISBN: 0-89296-087-6
Published by The Mysterious Press
                129 West 56th Street
                New York, NY 10019

Cover design by Denise Schultheis at the Angelica
    Design Group Ltd.
Cover illustration by Joel Iskowitz

Printed in the United States of America

For The Rashkows:
Sara, Steve, Sheri, Doug and Dean

"Oh, my dear, if you only knew how strange is the matter regarding which I am here, it is you who would laugh. I have learned not to think little of anyone's belief, no matter how strange it may be. I have tried to keep an open mind; and it is not the ordinary things of life that could close it but the strange things, the extraordinary things, the things that make one doubt if they be mad or sane."

—Dr. Van Helsing in Bram Stoker's *Dracula*

CHAPTER ONE

A pudgy vampire with a soiled black cape sat on a coffin across from me sipping a bottle of Hires Root Beer through a soggy straw. His loose fangs kept slipping, and each sip brought a sound somewhere between an asthmatic whistle and terminal pneumonia. He was fascinating, but so were the other four black-caped vampires who surrounded my client in that damp basement. My client, wearing a conservative gray suit and a fixed, uncomfortable smile, used his cigar to keep the vampires at bay, but they weren't to be denied, especially one white-faced woman with long raven hair parted down the middle.

"But Mr. Lugosi," she panted, "When are you going to play a vampire again?"

Lugosi shrugged enormously, playing to his rabid audience. He was almost sixty and looked every bit of it and more. His face was puffy and white, his smile a broad *V*. He didn't want to be here, but since he was, he couldn't resist the urge to perform.

"Lou-go-she," he corrected the woman, "Bay-lah Lou-go-she, but, my dear, that is of no importance. As to when I will play a vampire again, well, my friends," he sighed, and the *well* came out "vell," his familiar accent lying like goulash over his words. He took longer to get those last three words out than a doctor with bad news.

"One does what one must to make a living," he went on, with eyes closed to show how the burden of paying the grocer and the milkman had forced him into artistic compromise. "I would luff to do Dracula again, but . . ." he pointed to the cracked gray ceiling a few feet above his head, "to do it right. Ah, I know so much more now my friends, so much more."

"Hell," said a short Chinese vampire with a disappointing lack of accent and sympathy, "the only things you've played for five years are mad doctors who get torn up in the last reel."

"Dying," said Lugosi with a shake of his head, "for me is a living."

It was a punch line he had surely delivered before, but it brought no smiles from this group. Lugosi cast a secret look of exasperation at me. They weren't going for his best material, and he wanted to be rescued, but I wasn't ready to leave yet. I gurgled some Pepsi from my bottle, shifted on my coffin, and scooped up a handful of Saltines with my free hand.

We were in the lair of the Dark Knights of Transylvania, not very far below a fake-adobe neighborhood movie theater in Los Angeles in January of 1942. Both the theater and the neighborhood were rotting rapidly around this quintet of black-clad dreamers drooling over the memory of a ten-year-old movie, trying to savor the fantasy of evil immortality while the proof of the bankruptcy of that fantasy stood before them in the decaying form of a worn-out Hungarian actor who had seen better days and better cigars.

If they had bothered to look at me, which they didn't, the Dark Knights of Transylvania would have seen further evidence of the mortality of the human body. In almost forty-five years of being unable to make up my mind about what I planned to be when I grew up, I had picked up a hopelessly flat nose, a face that had been polite to too many punches, two bullet scars (three if you wanted to count the exit wound of one of them), and a large but as yet still finite number of lacerations caused by gun butts, broken bottles, assorted pieces of wood, an unopened jar of Jeris hair tonic, and such worldly weapons as knives and brass knuckles. My brain is barely protected by scar tissue, and my back pops out more often than champagne corks at a Tommy Manville wedding. Such things are more or less visible to the keen eye of even your novice vampire. What couldn't be seen was the fact that I'm a private detective with nothing in the bank but a bad credit rating, nothing in the world but a questionable reputation, and nothing on my mind but hard memories.

I had failed as a Glendale cop and a Warner Brothers security guard and I had only twenty-five bucks and an overdue bill on my office rent to show for nearly half a dozen years as a private investigator. Look at me, vampires. There are some bodies you can't get blood out of.

Amid the orgy of crackers, root beer, and Pepsi, I was trying to do the job I had been hired for by Lugosi. Someone had been playing games with him for over a month, sending messages written in animal blood through the mail saying, "He who mocks the vampire deserves his fate," and "Respect what you represent or suffer for it," or who ever can forget my own favorite, "Dignity or death." It was an old story in Los Angeles. Movie people often found themselves a fan they could do without. Cecil B. DeMille had a guy who even jumped into his dining room once and ruined the cream of turnip soup. The cops locked the guy up, but he escaped and came back to DeMille from time to time like a truly irate critic.

Lugosi's topper had been a hat box delivered to his home one morning. Inside the hat box was a cute little bat with a tiny stake through its heart.

Lugosi had shrugged this off as a sick prank. He'd pulled enough of them himself and had had them pulled on him. But

Lugosi had told the tale to a fellow Hungarian over a few drinks, and the Hungarian, who was an extra at Universal, mentioned it to Boris Karloff. Karloff had called me. He was worried about Lugosi. The world was exploding. The Japanese had just hit Pearl Harbor. The Germans were marching through Russia, and everyone was scared as hell. No one else was going to worry about Lugosi. With the world melting outside your window and the front pages a series of horror stories, the bottom had dropped out of the monster movies for a while. Lugosi had hit hard times, according to Karloff. He had lost his car and his home and a lot of his dignity. Lugosi was making a small comeback, but his body and his nerves had taken a hell of a beating.

"I'm afraid, Mr. Peters," Karloff had lisped deeply over the phone, "Bela resents what he sees as my greater success. I assure you it is only a relative success, but I seem to have adjusted much better to the inevitable life of evil into which I have been cast. Actually, I'm quite grateful to be typecast and working steadily. Would it be possible to approach Bela without mentioning me?"

With no client on the books and a stomach that echoed a cry for tacos and an occasional beer, I told him I'd give it a try. The try came the next afternoon when I called Lugosi and made an appointment, being as vague as I could about the reason. Lugosi's house was a small frame one-story with a little grass in front where he was playing quoits with a four-year-old neighbor.

"I'm Peters," I had told him, "Toby Peters. I'm a private investigator."

"And you sell your surfaces door-to-door and by telephone?" he had asked with an exaggerated raising of his eyebrows.

"I understand you've had some trouble. Someone playing tricks that might not be funny."

"I'll hide. You find me," the boy interrupted.

"No," glowered Bela, raising the sleeve of his gray cardigan sweater to his face like a cape. The boy was neither frightened nor impressed.

"Claire couldn't find me," said the boy.

"Not now," Lugosi said in mock menace.

"I'm going to the potty and having some cookies," replied the boy, who ran toward the house next door.

"Perhaps," said Lugosi with a small smile, "one should consider a new profession when he cannot frighten impressionable small children."

I made my pitch, something like the one you get from the exterminators who tell you if you don't hire them today, you'll be up to your ass in multiplying roaches by tomorrow afternoon. I told of the dangers of cranks and the troubles I'd seen. I gave him references and my lowest rate, fifteen a day plus expenses. I did everything but tell him if he didn't hire me I couldn't pay for the gas to get me back to my office.

"Mr. Peters," he had said, fishing a cigar from the pocket of his sweater, "the world is at war and I am not a wealthy man. The war will someday end, and the fool who sends dead bats will grow tired and move on to tormenting alley cats."

"Who opened the hat box with the bat?" I tried.

"I did," he said, lighting the cigar. "But I see what you are doing." His smile broadened as he got the cigar going and worked a gray foul cloud into the air over his head. "You are trying to frighten me. But that is my business, frightening people. Both my friend with the bat and you could be much more effective if *you* hired *me.*"

"Did you tell the police?"

"They thought it was a publicity trick."

I nodded knowingly. The odds were that I had Lugosi hooked. He had already invested time talking to me and listening to my pitch, and he hadn't made up some reason to kiss me off and fade indoors. He might be saying "no," but "maybe" was in view and "yes" only a length behind.

I pushed on. I needed the job. The few hundred I had picked up in a case I worked for Howard Hughes had gone for minimal repairs on my 1934 Buick and to my sister-in-law Ruth. The Buick still needed a paint job. It was—or once had been—a dark green but had taken some scars of its own that I'd patched up with green house paint five shades too light that I'd picked up in the basement of my rooming house. Now the car looked like an ad for moldy pigeon eggs. Children pointed to it in the street and it wasn't worth a damn for following anyone. A blind man could spot the old bomb in a blackout. The money to Ruth had been a secret from my brother Phil, a Los Angeles cop who wouldn't have taken it in spite of his mortgage, his three kids, and a salary that wouldn't keep a Tenth Avenue rummy in Cresta Blanca. If Phil found out about the money, he'd probably show his gratitude by tearing me apart and shoving me up his unpaid-for chimney the way Lugosi's ape had done to the old lady in *Murders in the Rue Morgue.*

After I spent ten more minutes on nonstop talking and watching Lugosi pollute the San Fernando Valley with his cigar, the boy next door came out to announce that he was going to sit on Lugosi's head.

"Mr. Peters," Lugosi said, clamping the cigar between his teeth and stooping slowly on one knee to accept the leap of the child, "you are hired for one week."

The kid clambered up Lugosi's back, and I reached out to give Lugosi a hand up. He rose with a pant and spoke around his cigar.

"Reach into my back pocket," he said. "Take thirty dollars advance out."

I did and returned the wallet.

"Call me tomorrow," he said, turning with the kid clinging to him.

"You have any gum?" the boy said as I turned my back.

"Perhaps," came back Lugosi's Hungarian accent, which answer both the kid and I knew could easily be turned into a yes.

The next day while I was sitting at my desk listening to the dental drill in the outer office and trying to think of where to start and what to have for lunch, Lugosi had called to report another letter in blood. This one said: "Do not attend the Dark Knights of Transylvania or your next."

Aside from lousy spelling, it was a place to start. Lugosi said he had, in fact, received an invitation in the same mail to attend a "sabbath" ceremony of the Dark Knights on the following night. The invitation had been on a small white card with a black bat embossed at the top.

"So?" he said.

"So, we go to the sabbath and I try to figure out which Dark Knight has been sending you mail."

And that was how I came to be seated on a coffin, trying to listen to a conversation ten feet away while a pudgy vampire sipped, slurped, and crunched in my face.

"Why don't you take your fangs out?" I suggested.

The vampire stopped sipping and put a finger from his right hand up to his mouth to keep the fangs from falling out as he spoke.

"I wouldn't look like a vampire if I took the fangs out," he answered reasonably.

"Right," I said, without adding that at best he looked like Elmer Fudd doing a vampire act.

"The fangs do throw my bite off," he confessed confidentially, leaning toward me.

"I know a dentist who might be able to help you," I said. "Name's Shelly Minck. We share an office downtown in the Farraday Building over on Hoover near Ninth."

Elmer Fudd said he thought he might look Shelly up and proved his good intentions by groping under his cape for a pencil to get the address. Shelly would like this. How many dentists could say they treated a vampire for fang overbite?

"My name is Count Sforzni," Elmer Fudd said, shifting his left hand to his mouth so he could extend his little balloon hand to shake mine. "We didn't meet when you came in because I was upstairs preparing the refreshments."

He nodded at the refreshments at the end of his coffin.

They included a dish of straight Saltines, a pitcher of water, a few bottles of tepid soda pop, and a quart of cheap wine.

"We don't usually prepare much," he confided. "Most of the Knights won't eat or drink at meetings. Vampire purists."

"My name's Peters. Your name is really Count Sforzni?"

"Well," he said, between rattling his fangs above the hub-bub of conversation nearby. "I'm Count Sforzni here. You know, honorary title. My name upstairs is Sam Billings. This is my theater." He let his eyes float upward to indicate the space over us.

Although the lights had been out in the theater when we came in, I had been able to make out the lobby posters for the current triple feature, *Host to a Ghost, Revolt of the Zombies,* and *Murder in the Red Barn.*

"Nice theater," I said, shifting my weight on the hard coffin. I reached back to see whether I had picked up a splinter and tried to catch a bit more of the Lugosi conversation.

"They're real," Billings-Sforzni whispered with what I took for pride.

"The fangs?" I whispered back.

"No," he said, pointing to my rear. "Coffins. I bought them at a funeral supply place. Read about them in *Casket and Sunnyside,* the undertakers' trade journal. Real bargains. Add to the atmosphere."

The atmosphere of the basement could be described as storefront funeral parlor with pieces of old theater lobby thrown in. Besides three coffins there was a small table with a black cloth over it and six candles burning on it. Three walls were gray and bare with a few movie posters, *Dracula, White Zombie,* and *The Black Cat,* covering holes or looking like they were pasted up by a drunk. The fourth wall, the one against which Lugosi had been trapped, was covered by heavy, blood-red, and very worn velvetlike drapes.

"Nice place," I told Billings, whose bald pate was doubly red from shyness or heat in the weird light and the air rapidly turning to atmospheric fog from Lugosi's cigar.

Lugosi caught my eye, a massive false smile on his face, and nodded toward the door in a way that would make it clear even to the Frankenstein monster that he wanted out.

"How many members are there in the Dark Knights?" I asked as innocently as I could, which was not very innocently, considering that I look like the pug who stands behind Edward G. Robinson in Warners gangster movies. You know the guy I mean, the one who never talks, looks like an ex-welterweight, and sticks his chin out every once in a while to show he's earning his living.

"We're a secret, very exclusive organization," Billings said, defensively reaching for a handful of crackers.

"You mean there's just the five of you?" I said with a friendly smile.

He fanged some crackers and gave a small nod to show I had calculated correctly.

One of the four vampires around Lugosi looked over at me. He was tall and dark, the most formidable-looking member of the group. I looked back at him with my innocent brown eyes and a mouth full of warm Pepsi. He turned slowly away.

"Are you interested in joining?" Billings said eagerly.

"I don't know." I shifted my weight on the coffin to reach for the last of the crackers. Billings' hand indicated the impulse to race me for the remnants, but courtesy and the possibility of new blood stayed his chunky grasp.

"These people are the only ones who know about the meetings?"

Billings put down his now-finished Hires, stifled a burp, and said, "We are secret and exclusive."

I turned my head to the group of vampires and Lugosi, whose eyes moved from his tormentors to me to the door.

"Can you tell me who everyone is?" I said, looking casually around and trying not to choke on my cracker.

"Certainly," said Billings. "There's Baroness Zendelia, Sir Malcolm."

"No," I pushed in. "Their real names."

"No," Billings countered, sitting up to his full five foot five. "That is private. Our human identities must remain secret."

"Then how do you mail notices to them?" I tried, but Billings had other things on his mind.

"Well . . . you think these coffins are a bit hard? I've thought of putting cushions on them, but it might look too tacky."

"How about red velvet?" I suggested.

"Maybe," Billings sighed, unconvinced, as he looked at the empty cracker dish.

Lugosi was clearly trying to break through the ring of bodies, and I considered the possibility of following the most likely suspect in the group but gave it up. The odds were too slim, the hour too late, and my gas too low. Lugosi made his way through the group and advanced toward me. I stood up and Billings joined me, almost falling back on his coffin.

"Whose idea was it to invite Mr. Lugosi tonight?" I asked Billings loud enough for the others to hear and tried to make it sound like the start of a thank-you-for-the-lovely-evening. Lugosi was at my shoulder listening, the quartet of fluttering capes in pursuit.

"I don't recall," said Billings, playing with his fangs.

"It was mine," whispered the dark woman, her voice somewhat foreign, amused, and a little sleepy. She stared immodestly at my much-traveled neck and I pulled up my collar.

"No," interjected a lean vampire with a jagged nose and a too-small cape that choked his words into a crimson gasp. His accent was definitely more New York Jewish than Transylvanian.

"No, no," came in the Chinese vampire, billowing his broad cape and elbowing his way to the foreground. The cape was so long that he stepped on it and tripped forward into Lugosi.

The tall dark vampire who had been looking at me earlier was the only one who didn't try to take any credit.

"Anybody oppose the invitation?" I tried, knowing no one would admit it in Lugosi's presence but hoping vampire competition would emerge.

"No, why?" asked the Chinese guy.

"Because," Lugosi said with a broad smile. "I like to be welcome. And I half-enjoyed our visit, but the sands of time fall relentlessly and the dawn approaches." Lugosi pointed in the general direction of the dawn somewhere above the moldy ceiling. We headed for the stairs, the vampires behind us. I could feel the warm breath of the woman behind me, and I imagined her eyes on my not-too-clean collar.

They escorted us up the narrow stairs, through the theater lobby and to the door, where hands reached out to pass me my coat and Lugosi his coat and Homburg hat.

We exchanged thanks, well wishes, invitations, undying love, and promises to be pen pals before we opened the door.

"Good night," Lugosi said over his shoulder and stepped into the cold darkness with me behind. In the past week, temperatures had hit lows of 29 and highs of 40. I had a coat from Hy O'Brien's Clothes for Him on Hollywood. The coat had been a bargain. I got it for only three bucks more than I had sold it to Hy for a month earlier.

There was no sky and almost no light. Blackout conditions had cut off the street lights and most businesses didn't keep a night light. They didn't want the first Japanese bombs to land on their taco stands. We stood there for a few seconds, trying to adjust to the darkness, and then I started toward my car, but there were no footsteps behind me. I turned and made out Lugosi's shape a dozen feet away.

"My hat," he whispered.

At first I thought he had said, "My bat," and considered the possibility that he had gone stark raving cuckoo, but he repeated it and I got it straight.

"It's in your hand," I said.

"And there is something in it," he answered. My eyes were

beginning to pick out little details now, like the trembling of his hands. I moved fast to his side and took the hat. I reached inside it and touched what felt like a sticky piece of cloth. I led Lugosi quickly to my car, got him in, and went around to get in on the other side. I started the engine and flipped on the overhead light. A lone car went down the deserted street, and we waited for it to pass before we looked down at the piece of black cloth I had pulled from the hat. The writing was in blood or a good imitation.

"It says, 'You were warned,' " I told Lugosi, who was recovering a bit from the shock. I flipped off the light. His face was hidden but I heard a sound like a laugh and then his familiar voice.

"Worthy of a Monogram serial," he said.

"Well," I said putting the car in gear. "We've got our list of suspects down to five. We're making progress."

As I drove Lugosi back home, I kept him talking, about his life, his work, anything to get the world back to normal.

"Once," he said, "I had ambition." I glanced over at him to see the light from passing cars cast dark shadows on his face. "I was in the National Theater of Hungary. I played Shakespeare. Can you imagine? I played Romeo. I was distinguished, yes. I was an officer in the Forty-third Royal Hungarian Infantry in the war. Wounded. I saw real death. And here a foolish trick makes me tremble."

"I've had better days myself," I tried.

"No, Mr. Peters, I live on hope. I have made less money than people think, have spent more than I should have on vanity and foolishness."

I was about to try to console him further when he laughed and elbowed me gently.

"No," he said, "I try, but I can't see myself as a tragic character. I've had good times. Let's stop for a drink. I have to be at the studio at eight in the morning, but tonight, my new friend, we share a bottle and tell our life stories and fill them with lies and truth and romance."

We went to a little bar I know on Sprina. Lugosi mixed beer and scotch and I nursed two beers for an hour. He stood drinks for everyone and listened to the bartender tell us that he heard MacArthur had been wounded and Manila had fallen. Another guy with a black wig that tilted to the side added that he heard the Army was going to start taking cars away from civilians because there was a shortage of vehicles.

Lugosi listened with a patient smile to the war gossip and the background jukebox playing Tommy Dorsey's version of "This Love of Mine."

I thought my client was far away from thoughts of bloody messages, but he looked into the last drops of amber scotch at the bottom of his beer mug and said softly,

> "But first on earth, as Vampyre sent,
> Thy corpse shall from its tomb be rent;
> Then ghastly haunt thy native place,
> And such the blood of all thy race . . ."

His words trailed off and then came back as the record stopped. Lugosi's voice rose slightly and the half-dozen guys in the bar and the barkeeper went silent.

> "Thy gnashing tooth, and haggard lip;
> Then stalking to thy sullen grave
> Go—and with Ghouls and Afrits rave,
> Till these in horror shrink away
> From spectre more accursed than they."

That pretty well killed the party. I got Lugosi home without any further conversation, promised to follow up on the Dark Knights, and left him in front of his door. I couldn't bring myself to ask him for another day's pay in advance.

CHAPTER TWO

Gunther Wherthman was a little over three feet tall, a genuine midget. At eight in the morning on January 3, 1942 he sat across from me slowly eating a poached egg. I could tell the time not from my watch, which was always an hour or two off, but from the Beech-Nut gum clock on my wall. I had received the clock in payment for returning a runaway grandmother to a guy who owned a pawn shop on Main Street. The job took ten minutes. Grandma was hiding in her closet.

Gunther wore a dark blue suit with not a wrinkle showing and a dark blue tie with some discreet light blue stripes running at a slight angle. He smelled of toilet water and looked ready to go to work, which he was. Work, however, was in the boarding-house room he lived in next to mine. There was little chance that Gunther, who made a modest living as a translator of German, French, Dutch, Flemish, Spanish, and Basque, would meet anyone during the day except for me and our landlady, who would neither care nor notice what he wore.

Gunther had talked me into the rooming house on Heliotrope in Hollywood after I had gotten him off a murder charge about a year earlier. The murder had been of a guy who played a Munchkin in *The Wizard of Oz*. Gunther, like most people under four feet tall in the Western world, had been in the movie. In fact, he had picked up a few dollars from time to time doing bit parts in movies that needed little people.

One of his favorite movie jobs had been to simply walk back and forth at the end of a long corridor past another midget. The director's idea was that no one would notice that the two men were midgets at that distance, and the corridor would look twice as long. Gunther had never bothered to see the movie.

It was Saturday morning and I planned to work, but first I gobbled an oversize bowl of Kix with brown sugar and drank a couple of cups of freshly brewed Schilling coffee I had picked up at Ralph's for twenty-nine cents a pound.

I discovered that Roosevelt was pushing for war plants to be moved away from the coast because they were vulnerable and that the Russians were holding the Germans sixty-five miles from Moscow in a place called Maloyaroslavets. Corregidor was preparing for a full-scale Japanese attack. Tony Martin had joined the Navy and Hank Greenberg had reenlisted. I found a photograph of Warner Brothers staging an air raid rehearsal. A bunch of sandbags surrounded Mike Curtiz, Dennis Morgan, Bette Davis, "George the Grip," Irene Manning, and Chet, a worker I recognized from my days at the studio. I showed the photograph to Gunther, who put down his spoon, examined it politely, and nodded.

"And this case is an important one?" Gunther said precisely, when his mouth was empty.

"Well," I answered, "it'll pay a few bills, but I think it's small time, which is just what I'll be happy with. Dime-a-dozen case of a nut writing a few letters, pulling a few tricks. I'll probably track him down in a few days, throw a scare, and earn my money."

Gunther didn't ask for details. He wiped his mouth with a

napkin and climbed down to clean up the meal while I helped myself to another bowl of Kix and made a mental note to pick up a few boxes of Wheaties, which were on sale for ten cents. Life, I thought, could be so simple.

My back hadn't given me any trouble for weeks. My sinuses were backed up as they had been for years by my crushed nose, but aside from a few headaches there was no trouble. The bone chip in the little finger of my left hand had shifted, but a few aspirin had helped me to forget it. I had had no migraine since November. The world was full of promise and hope, if you discounted the war.

I had eaten breakfast in my undershirt, not from any desire to offend Gunther, but to preserve the thin veneer of respectability that clung to my shirt, tie, and jacket. With a tight budget, I couldn't afford cleaning, and I sure as hell couldn't borrow a shirt from Gunther.

I kicked the mattress I slept on into the corner, got dressed, promised Gunther I'd pick up some Rinso and Horlick's malted milk, and went out the door and down the stairs as quietly as I could to avoid our deaf landlady, Mrs. Plaut, whose conversations would reduce an FBI agent to creamed spinach.

The newspapers had stopped printing the weather in case it might help the Japanese invasion plans. I had guessed that the day wouldn't be much warmer than the one before, and I had been right. Being right had simply meant bringing my coat with me. I had only a lighter-weight suit to change into, and that was even dirtier than the one I was wearing.

With twenty bucks of Lugosi's thirty left after groceries, gas, and an Old Nick candy bar, I drove downtown trying to decide whether to call Carmen and ask her to go to the Pantages with me that night after her shift behind the cash register at Levy's Grill. The Pantages was running a complete showing of *Ball of Fire* at 1:30 for defense workers and insomniacs. I was still considering the possibility when I got to the Farraday Building and parked in a spot I know in an alley behind a garbage can. There was always a chance that someone might mistake my heap for discarded scrap, but I risked it.

The lobby of the Farraday was deserted except for Jeremy Butler, the former wrestler, present poet, and landlord, who was using his considerable muscle and a can of Old Dutch cleanser to get some scribbling off the gray wall next to the building directory. The scribbling was vaguely obscene, but some people thought the directory was even worse. We had a bookie posing as a smoke shop, a half-mad doctor who specialized in treating cases he didn't report, a baby photographer who was even uglier than me and who never carried a camera, a con man named Albertini who changed the name of his company every week (this week it was Federal Newsprint, Ltd.), and a variety of others including Sheldon Minck, DDS, and Toby Peters, the far side of the detective business.

"How's business, Toby?" Butler said. His sleeves were rolled up for the task, and his arms bulged under fields of black hair.

"Got a client," I said pausing to try to read what he was erasing but having no luck. "Bela Lugosi. Say, you're a poet. You know a poem that starts 'But first on earth as Vampyre sent?'"

"It's not the beginning," Butler said, attacking what looked like the remnants of an anatomical drawing. "It's by Lord Byron. He was screwy about vampires. A lot of poets like that stuff. I even wrote a vampire poem." He stepped back to examine his efforts, didn't like what he saw, and went back to the wall with cold determination.

"It was published in Little Bay Review last year," he said.

"Terrific," I answered and started to move into the darkness and toward the stairs, but his voice, grunting with each scrub, came at me with the poem. I stopped politely to listen.

> "Whatever happened to yellow?
> Did it bleed to green and mellow

to almost white from the gentle bite
of a grass-leaf vampire?
Yellow is seen
as the lack of green
by those who have never known
the dying moan
of a fire engine
or a grasshopper's life fluid.

"Yellow spins in men,
void not null
weightless though heavy.
I play myself in string quartets;
But I can hear
only two instruments of fear
in the present tense
echoing yellow."

And then, without a pause, "If I get my hands on the son-of-a-bitch who did this to my wall," he said evenly, "I'll make him pay."

"I'm sure you will," I said and headed for the familiar Lysol-smelling stairwell. Jeremy devoted his life to poetry and staying just ahead of the filth that would inevitably inherit the Farraday Building. Only a poet or a monster would have taken it on, and Jeremy was both. I didn't understand a word of his poem, and I didn't worry about it. The whole case had become too literary for me.

I was sure when I got to my office door that Shelly Minck was inside and that there was little chance he'd know a poem about vampires.

I eased through the tiny waiting room, trying not to disturb the dust, and made my way into Shelly's office. He was working on a fat woman who gave out low "argghh's" the entire time she was in the chair whether Shelly was working on her or not. His chubby fingers danced over the instruments, and he cleaned each one on his dirty once-white smock before he plunged it into the woman's mouth. Sweat poured from the fat at Shelly's neck, as it always did when he worked, and he paused between searches, probes, and seizures to take a puff at the cigar that he kept perched on his instrument tray.

"Hi, Shelly," I said, looking over his shoulder at the fat woman's decaying mouth. Her frightened eyes caught mine, and I tried not to grimace.

"Toby," he said, "I was hoping you'd come in today. You want to go in with me on a London-type bomb shelter? I can get it for two hundred eighty-five dollars, install it in my yard."

He pulled something small and bloody out of the fat woman's mouth and her "argghh" went up a few decibels.

"You're all right, Mrs. Lee," he said, examining the object curiously. "It was just a . . . a piece of something."

"What good would a bomb shelter do me in your yard?" I said. "I don't think the Japanese are going to give us enough warning to get me from Hollywood to Van Nuys if they attack."

"Mrs. Lee," he said, turning his eyes, myopic behind thick lenses, on his patient. "Do you think you and Mr. Lee, if there is a Mr. Lee, would be interested in half-interest in a bomb shelter? A heavy bomb could destroy all the work I've been doing on your mouth."

"Arrgghh," said Mrs. Lee, with terror in her massive eyes.

"She said yes," Shelly said, looking for an elusive instrument as he pulled at his cigar.

"I think she said no," I said.

Shelly shrugged, found a sharp instrument, tested it on his finger, and turned to Mrs. Lee, who drew back as deeply into the chair as she could.

"Relax," grunted Shelly, "it's clean."

I didn't want to watch. I went into my office and closed the door. The sound of Mrs. Lee's "argghh" shook my hinges, and I tried to ignore her by looking at the picture on the wall of my dad, my brother, me, and Kaiser Wilhelm, our dog. It was a photograph out of antiquity and it always soothed me and inspired me to new heights of provocation against the brother with whom I had been battling since the day I was born.

My mail didn't have much to offer besides an ad that said I could have dinner and hear Paul Whiteman at the Florentine Gardens for $1.75. That would be four bucks plus gas and a tip if I took Carmen. The Pantages was fifty cents, and we could pick up a couple of tacos for another dime each. If Lugosi paid me for another day, we could even have a couple of beers. Such were the plans of your well-known man-about-town.

There was an interesting message on the spindle on my desk. Shelly's hand was unmistakable and the number illegible, but I thought I recognized the name.

"Shelly," I yelled through the door when there was a lull in Mrs. Lee's agony, "is this message from Martin Leib?"

"Right," he shouted back.

Leib was a starched-collar, no-nonsense, old-timer lawyer with consulting contracts at the major studios. I'd worked with him once and knew if he was calling me it wasn't sentimental or to have a drink and tell tall stories. I found his number in the directory and called. He answered on the second ring.

"Peters," he said softly. "Your call came just as I was going to call someone else to handle this. I have a job for you, similar to the last one. Client accused of murder. Warners would like to keep things quiet until everything is clear. On my end, I can contain publicity for a few days at most. I need an investigation quickly and some solid information about what the police have and are doing. Can you handle it?"

If I told Leib I had a job and a client, he would say "Fine" and hang up. Besides, why couldn't a detective have two clients at a time? True, it had never happened to me before, but it came at a point when I could use all the help from capitalistic sources I could muster. Bela Lugosi's crank was intriguing, but a murder case for Warner Brothers was possibly big money.

"Fifty a day and expenses," I said. "Two days in advance."

"Thirty-five," said Leib. "This is for Jack Warner, not Louis Mayer. I'll have the money waiting for you at the Wilshire station where our client is being held. I think it best if you get to him immediately. I've already begun from my end."

"And?" I said, half thinking about the Florentine Gardens.

"And it doesn't look promising," he said. That was all we had to go with, so I finished the business at hand.

"Client's name?"

"Faulkner, William Faulkner."

"The writer?"

"The alleged murderer," said Leib and hung up.

Business was booming. A full year like this and I'd be challenging Pinkerton. I picked up my coat and went back into Shelly's office. He was demonstrating to Mrs. Lee how to rinse her mouth. She had lost all semblance of control and dumbly mocked Shelly's actions. Her "arrgghh" was down to a slow, low gurgle.

"I'm going on another case," I said to Shelly's back. He waved his cigar to let me know he had heard.

"Almost forgot," I added, heading for the door. "Guy named Billings might be getting in touch with you. He has an overbite problem from fangs."

That got Shelly, who turned around and squinted in my general direction through the bulletproof lenses of his glasses.

"He's a vampire," I explained.

Mrs. Lee seemed to hear the word *vampire* through her confused stupor and looked vaguely in my direction.

"Vampires are a dental impossibility," Shelly announced firmly. "At least vampires with fangs. There's no way the human jaw could support fangs." He put his finger into Mrs. Lee's mouth to demonstrate as he spoke. "Throw the whole mouth off. The guy'd look like Andy Gump or Mortimer Snerd, and his jaw . . . he wouldn't get a decent night's sleep or be able to eat."

"But vampires don't eat and they sleep like the dead during the day," I said.

Mrs. Lee nodded in agreement, and Shelly frowned at her.

"Mrs. Van Helsing here," he said derisively, pointing his thumb at the woman.

"Not a real vampire," I explained, opening the door. "Just a guy who wears fake fangs and likes dressing up. A little higher class than some of your patients."

"If he calls, I'll look at him," Shelly said professionally, turning to Mrs. Lee. His glasses slipped down on his nose and his free thumb came up just in time to keep them from tumbling into Mrs. Lee's lap.

The Farraday Building had an elevator, and Jeremy Butler saw to it that the elevator went up and down, but there was nothing he could do to make it go up and down at a rate that most mortals found reasonable. I ran down the stairs, putting on my coat as I went and listening to the echo of my footsteps around me. On the floor below ours, the bookie was fumbling at the lock on his door. The phone was ringing on the other side and he was trying to get in before he missed a bet, but his eyes were bleary and the harder he tried, the more the lock resisted. I didn't bother to greet him.

Butler was still going at the wall with his second can of Old Dutch.

"Perhaps I should just paint the whole wall?" he asked.

"I think it looks fine," I said. Interior decoration wasn't my line, but the irregular patch of white he had worn into the gray wall made the lobby look like the set for a German horror movie.

A neighborhood derelict was pressing his nose to the window of my car when I hurried into the alley. He pulled his gray-stubble face away when he heard me and plunged his hands deep into his pockets, pretending to admire the scenery of the alley, the piles of garbage, the empty cartons. He tried to look as if he were waiting for a streetcar and succeeded in looking as if he had been caught with his claw in the bird cage.

I handed the guy a quarter, told him it was a nice day, and pulled out, heading the car up Hoover and across on Wilshire. Leib's office was in Westwood, even closer to the station than mine. There was a chance the advance would beat me to the door. In my greed, I had neglected to find out who Faulkner had murdered and why.

As I passed the shivering palms and the occasional people who had come to Los Angeles looking for what they couldn't find further east and finding what they hadn't looked for, I thought of the two times I had seen Faulkner. He had been laboring away at some project at Warners a few years earlier when I spotted him through the office window of a producer I was on a job for. Faulkner had looked sad and serious. His typewriter was giving him no fun. He was probably having even less fun today.

I found a space a few blocks from the station and jogged over. A young balding uniformed cop I knew named Rashkow almost knocked me back down the stone stairs.

"Hello," he said seriously.

"Hi, my brother in today?"

"He's in," Rashkow said, pulling his coat closed. "Just saw him. This is my last day."

"Vacation?" I asked.

"Army," he said. "I joined a week ago. The papers say things are going good, but I don't know."

"I don't know either," I said. "Good luck. Win the war fast."

"I'll try," said Rashkow, adjusting his blue cap as he lumbered down the stairs.

The damned war kept intruding on my life and profession. It was hard to concentrate on your career when all about you were losing their heads and blaming it on others.

The desk sergeant, an old timer named Coronet, motioned me over and handed me an envelope.

"Just came for you," he said, without taking his eyes off two silent Japanese kids about twenty who were handcuffed together on the bench in a corner.

"What'd they do?" I asked Coronet, whose hostility to the two took the form of a jutting lower lip and clenched fists.

"Woman sitting behind them at the Loew's heard them applauding Pearl Harbor during the newsreel and hissing Roosevelt," Coronet explained.

The two young men, both skinny and not sure whether to be scared or defiant, looked at Coronet and then at me.

"That's a crime?" I said.

"Sure it's a crime," Coronet said without taking his accusing eyes from the pair. "We're at war."

That didn't answer my question, but I knew I would get nothing more sensible from Coronet, and I had my envelope of money from Leib, so I went up the twenty creaking brown stairs and through the often-kicked wooden door at the top and into the squad room. The room smelled, as it always did, as all squad rooms always do, of food—old food, new food, hot food, cold food. The smell of food even overpowered the smell of humanity and stale smoke.

It was a slow day, but detectives were seated at some of the desks. A few were on telephones. One fat detective named Veldu was sitting on the corner of the desk of a new guy I didn't recognize. Veldu had a sandwich in one hand, coffee in the other, and a mouthful of philosophy for the new guy, whose hair was black and plastered down and parted in the middle as if he were about to try out for a barbershop quartet.

"So they rank Lem Franklin number two," Veldu was saying. "Number two. Can you imagine that? Buddy Baer, that schlob could crack him in a minute. There's maybe six guys who could take Franklin on a bad day." He chomped on his sandwich and put down his coffee so he could raise his fingers to indicate the six guys. "Bob Pastor, Melio Bettina, Abe Simon, Lou Nova, Roscoe Toles, even Tamy Mauriello. In fact,

Pastor should be number one and Conn should be down at the bottom. He's got no punch. Louis hasn't got feelings. He's got to be clubbed to death." With this, Veldu demonstrated with his fist against the desk how one would have to club Joe Louis. The desk shook and the coffee spilled.

"Shit," bellowed Veldu around a bite of sandwich. "I'll have to get another coffee." He lumbered away, leaving the mess for the new guy, who reached into a drawer for some Kleenex and tried to keep the stain from joining all the other stains. The new guy spotted me.

"What can I do for you?" he said impatiently, which was a bad sign in a new detective, at least bad for me and any potential criminals he might meet.

"My name's Peters," I said, reaching out a hand. "I'm a private investigator doing some legwork for a lawyer named Leib on a client you have locked up here, Faulkner. I'd like to see our client."

The new guy looked at my hand and went on cleaning his desk. I put my hand back at my side. The new guy didn't say anything. He just kept scrubbing. I looked over at a woman two desks away talking to another detective. She was well groomed, wearing a little hat with a tall feather and a two-piece suit with the skirt to the knees. Her shoulders were slightly padded, and she looked as if she had just been outfitted at I. Magnin.

". . . my ears," I heard her say and tried to listen to more, but the new guy was looking up at me with less than friendship and a pile of soggy Kleenex he didn't know what to do with.

"I'll see," he said, walking toward the office cubbyhole of Lieutenant Philip Pevsner in the corner. He dropped the Kleenex in a wastebasket, and a black kid about fifteen who was waiting to be interrogated inched away from him.

I tried to pick up more of the well-groomed woman's conversation. I thought I caught her saying "Sally Rand" to the cop, who listened patiently, but I wasn't sure. I didn't have time to hear more. The new cop motioned to me from Pevsner's doorway, and I moved through the random array of desks and bodies, stepping over feet and past secrets.

The new guy stood back with a sour look, and I went into the office giving him a raw "Thanks" over my shoulder.

"Friendly guy," I told Pevsner as the door closed.

"His name's Cawelti," Pevsner said without looking up from the file on the desk. "He did five years uniformed in Venice. He had troubles but he did the job. I like people who get the job done." Then he looked up at me. I knew the look of mild contempt I would get, but it was mixed with a recent touch of tolerance that was at best a sign of temporary peace. Phil was a little taller than me, a little broader, a few years older, and a lot heavier. His close-cut steely hair was a magnet for his thick, strong fingers. He scratched constantly, whether from dandruff, habit, or perplexity I was never sure, and I had seen him doing this for more than thirty years. He was my brother.

He sighed. That was the friendliest he could be to me. I responded by making no bad jokes. The war had brought us to a truce. I had even lost the chance to give my running rub of asking about his wife Ruth and the kids. I lost it by actually visiting them on December 7 and doing a rotten job of hiding the soft touch I was for his new baby, Lucy, who reduced me to stupid grins. Phil was almost fifty, too old for kids, like Lugosi, but since I didn't have any, I kept my mouth shut.

Phil wasn't too great at dealing with adults. His impulse was usually to use his fists. I had learned that as a kid and bore the nose to prove it. As a cop he had grown no more mellow. Crime was personal with him. Criminals ate into his free time, committed crimes just to make his life difficult, murdered, raped, and went on rampages just to keep him angry and busy. Being a cop wasn't just a job for Phil; it was a vendetta, a vendetta he could never win. There were a lot more of *them* than there were of him, and he usually associated me with the criminals, with working for potential and accused criminals.

Even if my clients proved to be innocent part of the time, according to Phil it wasn't worth the effort.

"You're working the Faulkner case?" he asked, looking back at his file.

"Right," I said.

"There's no case to work," he said, standing up and loosening his already loose tie. He tapped the thin file on the desk. "He did it. Two eyewitnesses, the victim's wife and the victim himself before he died."

"William Faulkner murdered someone?"

"I just said that," continued Phil, looking at me with growing impatience.

"Do you know who he is?" I asked.

Phil's face turned red, starting at his neck and going up.

"I'm busy, but I'm not illiterate," he said. "I don't give a crap and a holler if he's the pope." Phil pointed at me. "He did in a citizen and he's going up for it. Leib can pull his strings downtown, and you can pull your tricks, and this whole thing can stay tight for a few days, but it's going to blow and he is going over."

The rage that festered beneath Phil's uncalm exterior sometimes boiled into the air and threatened the closest person, who was frequently me.

"Hold it, Phil," I said soothingly. "I'm just doing a job."

"Read the report," he said with a grunt, "but don't sit behind my desk. I'm going out for a coffee. Cawelti will bring Faulkner up here."

"Thanks," I said to the closing door. It had been the most civil conversation I had had with my brother in years.

I picked up the file and pulled the report. The file had a few statements by witnesses and the coroner and a report by the detective in charge, Cawelti. I sat in the chair opposite Phil's desk and started to put my feet up, then remembered what had happened the last time Phil had caught me with my feet on his desk. I almost wound up two inches shorter, which I could ill afford. The report was good and Faulkner was surely in trouble.

"Report—Detective Officer John Cawelti, Wilshire.

"At 9:20 p.m. on January 3, 1942 I was called to 3443 Benedict Canyon in Beverly Hills. I arrived just after the ambulance. Doctor, Bengt Lidstrom of County, said victim, Jacques Shatzkin of that address, was dead. Three bullets in chest. Officer Steven Bowles was on site and said he had been called. Bowles (report attached) arrived before Shatzkin died. Shatzkin identified William Faulkner, writer, as his assailant. Camile Shatzkin, deceased's wife, also identified Faulkner. Jacques Shatzkin's identification was positive. Shatzkin was author's representative and had met previously with Faulkner. Faulkner had been invited for dinner to talk business. He arrived late, according to deceased and his widow, fired point-blank at Shatzkin, and then left. Though victim was unable to do no more than identify assailant, the wife said that she knew of no quarrel between the two, though husband had described Faulkner as moody during their one lunch meeting. Faulkner was picked up at the Hollywood Hotel at 10:10 p.m. He denied knowledge of Shatzkin murder or dinner invitation and was singularly uncooperative. He admitted having had lunch with Shatzkin two days earlier (Wednesday). Check with Shatzkin's office confirmed luncheon meeting on Wednesday with Faulkner. Search of Faulkner's hotel room, conducted 4:30 a.m. Saturday, January 4, with Sergeant Veldu present and two security officers from Warners, Lovell and Hillier, led to discovery of .38 caliber revolver, recently fired. Ballistics run indicates this was weapon used to kill Shatzkin. Faulkner charged with murder 7 a.m. Saturday, January 4, 1942. Asked to call lawyer, Martin R. Leib of Westwood. Made no further statement."

I had just finished the report when the door opened and Cawelti of the sleek dark hair ushered William Faulkner into the small office.

CHAPTER THREE

Faulkner was a wiry guy about my age and height with a small mustache and a chip on his shoulder the size of Catalina Island. He had a high-bridged, almost Indian nose with heavy-lidded, deep-set brown eyes. His face was tan and he held a blackened pipe in his thin lips. I couldn't tell what was going on in his head other than that he had a distaste for the room, the situation, me, and possibly life in general. His eyes seemed to show melancholy, calculation, and a private sense of humor at the same time, as if he saw himself as a tragic figure and accepted the role, maybe even welcomed it. I can't say I liked him immediately. I wondered whether he knew any vampire poems.

"Your client," Cawelti said, ushering Faulkner to the chair across from Phil's desk and backing out with feigned respect. Faulkner didn't sit. He didn't offer his hand. He took the pipe out of his mouth and examined me.

"Forgive my lack of social grace in these surroundings, Mister . . ."

"Peters," I said. "Toby Peters. Private investigator working for Martin Leib and, I guess, Warner Brothers on your behalf."

Faulkner's voice was a little deeper than I had expected and distinctly Southern. I was having trouble with my words, trying to be formal and knowing I was unnatural. He had that effect. Faulkner stood behind the chair playing with his pipe, and I walked over to the window behind Phil's desk and pretended to look out. Since it faced a brick wall four feet away and hadn't been cleaned for a generation or two, I couldn't see anything.

"I don't think they're going to give us a lot of time in here," I said, "so I'd appreciate it if you'd just tell your story."

I pulled out my notebook with the worn spirals. It had a few ragged pages left. I could finish up on the back of the letter in my pocket from a hotel in Fresno complaining that I owed them for a night's lodging from a lifetime or two ago. I turned my eyes to Faulkner, who looked as if he might be deciding to tell me to go to hell. An almost nonexistent move of his shoulder made me think he had chosen possible salvation over dignity. I almost wrote that down, but I didn't have enough paper and the nub of my pencil might not last long. I also thought I had stolen the line from the one Faulkner novel I had read.

"There is irony in your request," Faulkner said, examining his pipe for defects and appreciating the embers. "I've just delivered a collection of stories to my publisher, none of which is as bizarre as this. I was going to start by saying—as I told the police—that I have killed no one."

"I understand how you feel," I said, scratching away to visible lead with my grimy thumb so I'd have a pencil to work with.

"Unfortunately," Faulkner went on softly, "I don't need sympathy. I need professional help. My inclination is simply to be irate and insist on my release, but apparently someone has gone through quite an effort to make that impossible."

"You mean you think you've been framed?" I said, to stay in the conversation.

"Consider the alternative," he continued. "It is either that or else I have gone mad, which is certainly a possibility, given the state of the world, though I doubt my madness would manifest itself as an attack on an agent. I would be much more likely to attack a publisher. May I suggest we sit down?"

I nodded, and he sat in the chair across from the desk, leaving me Phil's chair in which I was forbidden to sit on pain of decapitation. I sat. It helped establish a client-professional air in the rancid room, and it gave me a little extra to worry about. Faulkner crossed his legs and examined the back of his right hand. My feet started to go up on the desk. I resisted and planted them on the wooden floor.

"My tale is simple," Faulkner began with clear distaste for the task. "I met Jacques Shatzkin but once, for lunch at that restaurant with the aquarium window on Sixth Street."

"Bernstein's Fish Grotto," I supplied. "Why did you meet?"

Faulkner shifted the ashes in his pipe with a thin finger, cleaned his finger on a handkerchief from his tweed jacket pocket, made sure his tie was in place, and spoke softly.

"He called me and said he wanted to discuss a business arrangement that might be reasonably lucrative for me. I have an agent, but Mr. Shatzkin has—had—a good reputation, and I am somewhat in need of money."

"May I . . ." I started, but stopped when I looked at Faulkner's face. It had turned slightly red.

"I do not suffer from false humility," he said, "or at least I so delude myself. I earned less than thirty-two hundred dollars last year. I have a home and a family, and I carry the burden of assumption on the part of the public that I am financially solvent as the result of a family estate that does not exist and enormous royalties that have never existed. I have had but one economic success."

"*Pylon,*" I tried. I had fond memories of the book. I had once hidden evidence, a pornographic photograph, in my copy.

"*Sanctuary,*" Faulkner corrected. "And the money from

that has been long dispersed. I am in Los Angeles to seek employment from Warner Brothers with the help of my agent and Mr. Howard Hawks. Mr. Warner, so far, has not seen fit to make me a generous offer, or a firm offer of any kind. I am inclined to accept whatever offer I may get. So, when Mr. Shatzkin called . . ."

"Where did he call you?" I asked.

"At my hotel, the Hollywood," said Faulkner, finding a match and getting his pipe going.

"He called you and you met at the restaurant?"

"We met at Mr. Shatzkin's office building," Faulkner puffed, "and then went to the restaurant where I had lobster *naturale* and he had a large shrimp salad. You have that?"

I wrote it down. In spite of Faulkner's sarcasm, it might be something to check. It might not be, probably wouldn't be, but you took what you could get and carried it. I was tempted to tell Faulkner to stick to his writing and let me stick to my job.

"Mr. Shatzkin offered me the rings of Saturn, the moon, and Biloxi," Faulkner went on. "I told him I would check with my agent and get back to him. We parted amicably outside the restaurant, and he promised to call me. He never did, and I never saw him again."

"And you never met Mrs. Shatzkin?"

"I never had that pleasure," he said sarcastically.

"How did Shatzkin seem?" I went on.

"Seem," Faulkner repeated, making it clear I had chosen the wrong word. "A bit too earnest, too fawning, too false, exactly what I expected in and of Hollywood."

"You own a gun?"

"Yes, several; they are all in Oxford, Mississippi, in my study at Rowan Oak. They are locked securely away; I have an eight-year-old daughter. I brought none with me. I did not expect to be attacked, nor to commit murder or robbery."

That did it. I put down the envelope I was writing on and looked up at him. I noticed that my legs had made their way up to the desk when I wasn't looking. The hell with it.

"Look, Mr. Faulkner, I've got a job to do and you want to stay alive and out of jail and the newspapers—at least I think you do. We're in the same boat. I need the money for this case. I'm reasonably good at what I do, but I'm also somewhat human. If you tickle me and don't hit scar tissue, I laugh. If you torture me and hit an old wound, I cry."

"I recognize the allusion," Faulkner said, "and appreciate the point. I will try to be more civil, but the circumstances do affect my behavior. It is not just my life, but the world that is bitched proper this time, isn't it? I'd like to be dictator now. I'd take all Congressmen who refused to make military appropriations and I'd send them to the Philippines. On this day a year from now I don't think there'll be one present second lieutenant alive. And here we are playing games with a meaningless murder, and I sit a helpless . . . forgive me, Mr. Peters, but perhaps you can better understand my emotions."

"Apology accepted," I said. I didn't exactly like him now, but at least he seemed like a human being instead of a Southern imitation of George Sanders. "The shooting took place at nine or so last night. Where were you?"

"As I told the officer who brought me in here," he said, drawing on his pipe to regain his calm exterior, "I was working with a writer named Jerry Vernoff. We were in my hotel room. My agent, Bill Herndon, and I had agreed to try to work up a story treatment for Warners as a preliminary step to possible employment. Mr. Vernoff has worked extensively on story treatments for various studios and has a reputation for working quickly and commercially. I believe someone at Warners suggested the possible collaboration. We ate dinner at the hotel."

"Which makes it unlikely that you would have had a dinner appointment with Shatzkin," I concluded. He nodded in agreement. I didn't have a pinhead of an idea what was going on, but I had some names to work with. I put the notebook and envelope in my pocket and was about to order my feet off the desk when the door came open. If I had been listening to the waves of voices and sounds in the outer squad room instead of getting absorbed in my job, I might have heard Phil's Franken-stein tread, but such was not to be.

Phil looked at Faulkner and then at me, and he turned as red as the ketchup stain on his shirt. Behind him, Cawelti stood in anticipation of something he could see expanding in my brother like a berserk balloon, something that had to come out or explode. My right foot had fallen asleep or I would have forced it down, but I couldn't move it. Phil took the one step from the door to the desk, his double-ham of a hand descend-ing in slow motion. I watched in fascination as it hit my right knee, spinning me out of the chair and against the wall. I sank to the floor with Phil taking another step toward me, and then Faulkner's voice broke over his shoulder.

"Pardon me, Lieutenant," he said, "but you seem to have the scenario wrong. I was under the impression that the police beat up the suspects, not their lawyers' representatives."

Phil paused and looked back at Faulkner, who met his eyes and held them. That lasted long enough for me to scram-ble to my feet, but my knee was sore and almost gave way. Cawelti stood in the door with a touch of smirk on his face. Phil caught the look out of the corner of his eye and realized he was surrounded by adversaries. Normally, he would have bulled his way through all three of us, breaking Faulkner first like a twig, stomping on Cawelti, and saving me for something special, but time had mellowed Phil and he settled for, "Get your asses out of here, fast, all of you."

I hobbled to the door as Phil bumped past me, sat down in his now-contaminated chair, and stuck his head into the Faulk-ner file. Faulkner followed me slowly, and Cawelti closed the door behind us.

"He's my brother," I explained to Faulkner.

Faulkner nodded knowingly and replied, "Yes, I too have had brothers."

That struck me as a strange way of stating things, but I didn't question it. I was suddenly aware that the entire squad room was quiet and faces were aimed in our direction. At first I thought it might be recognition of Faulkner. Then I realized that Phil had made one hell of a noise throwing me against the wall. The silence lasted a couple of beats, and then everyone went back to his or her own private world.

"I'll be in touch with Mr. Leib as soon as I have anything," I told Faulkner. There was no point in telling him to take it easy or that everything would be all right, that I would take care of his problems and Bela Lugosi's and save Corregidor within two days. I wasn't even sure I could make it to my car on my wounded knee.

Cawelti led the way for Faulkner, and the two disappeared through the haphazard maze of desks. I tried to hide my limp as I eased over to a familiar face, that of Sergeant Steve Seidman, who was looking up at me as I made my way to his desk. He was a thin, white-faced, sandy-haired cadaver of a cop in a gray suit, the only suit I had ever seen him wear. Maybe he had a closet full of duplicates. Seidman was the closest thing my brother had to a partner. Seidman's strength was his inability to be ruffled. His idiosyncracy was his genuine respect for Phil.

"How's it going, Toby?" he said as I leaned against his desk, trying to hide a grimace of pain or turn it into something resembling a smile. A uniformed cop ambled past me with an old man manacled to his wrist. The old man gave me a toothless grin. On Seidman's desk was an ugly chunk of metal vaguely the shape of a club. Seidman saw me looking at it.

"Got that from a medical student at USC," he explained. "A guy tried to mug him and his girlfriend. Med student picked up this handy-dandy all-purpose piece of junk from the gutter and exposed the guy's brain with it. Broad daylight. Cop across the street in a diner saw the tail end and held off long enough to gulp his coffee. If he had moved a little faster, he could have saved the mugger a lot of surgery and me a lot of work."

"The point?" I asked.

"Phil has a lot of cases on his mind," he said.

"Phil is fifty and will never be more than a lieutenant," I said. "Surliness is a way of life for him. He's at war and the world is full of enemies, including me."

"Maybe so," sighed Seidman. I looked into the eyes in his sunken face. They were as black and faraway as the night sky. There was no distinction between the iris and the pupil. It was one wide, deep circle to infinity.

"Faulkner," I said, above the start of an argument in a distant corner. The manacled old man had punched the cop in the kidney, and the cop had restrained himself admirably, limiting his wrath to one elbow in the old guy's stomach and a lot of shouting. Seidman looked over at the conflict without emotion and spoke to me.

"Cawelti's case," he said. "Looks like a tight one. One live witness. One dead man who identified the killer. One gun found in Faulkner's hotel room. Who could ask for more?"

"I could," I said.

Seidman's voice went down so that I could hardly hear it.

"So could Cawelti," he said. "He's not looking into corners. Wants to wrap this up tight, get his name in the papers, a pat on the head from Phil, and a nice note in his personnel file."

"What about Faulkner's alibi?" I tried, looking around for the well-groomed lady, but she was gone.

"That writer, Vernoff, says Faulkner went out alone for a drink just before nine," Seidman said. "Plenty of time to pump a few drinks into himself and a few shots of something more deadly into Shatzkin and hurry back to the hotel."

"Something sound wrong with that to you?" I said.

Seidman shrugged. "Hell of a complicated way to commit a murder. No motive." Seidman's eyes moved up and over toward Phil's door behind my back. I could sense the hulking presence of my brother behind me. I got off Seidman's desk and limped toward the squad room door. I got four feet before

Phil's hand grabbed my left shoulder. I turned, wondering what he had in store for me this time.

"This has been a hell of a week," he said. as quietly as he could, which was not very quiet. It was as close as he had ever come to an apology.

"They all are," I said.

"They all are," he agreed and turned to stalk back into his office.

The two Japanese kids were still on the bench waiting for someone to take them away and shoot them for treason. Coronet, the desk sergeant, was keeping his eye on them to the point where a good lightfinger could have taken his gun, his uniform, and the rusty fixtures of the Wilshire station without his knowing it. My knee throbbed, but I made it across the tile floor and out the door into the cold. In my pocket was a comfortable advance from Martin Leib and a few notes. I went to the drugstore at the corner, got some coffee and a second breakfast of Shredded Wheat, and tried to decide what to do next.

The waitress, who recognized me from previous visits and probably thought I was a cop from down the street, served me quietly, but her radio blasted the news behind her. Corregidor was beating back the Japanese, and the Nazi drive into Russia was being stalled by bad weather and angry Russians. Dorothy Thompson was getting a divorce from Sinclair Lewis, and the Joe Louis/Buddy Baer rematch was definitely going to be covered on the radio. It was too hard to think, and I had too many things to think about. I needed a new notebook and some toothpaste. I picked up a can of Pepsodent tooth powder for thirty-nine cents and for another ten cents got Bob Hope's book *They Got Me Covered* as a premium. I figured I'd go home, soak my knee in the bath, and let Hope cheer me up while I decided what to do next.

I got into my specked Buick, ground it into gear, and made for Wilshire, dropping the idea of Carmen and the Florentine Room. My intentions shifted. The next day was Sunday. Maybe

I'd take my two nephews Nate and Davey to see *Dumbo*. At least that's what I'd tell Phil and Ruth. I would really take them back to Billings's adobe theater for *Host to a Ghost* and *Revolt of the Zombies*. I knew I could trust the boys to tell a lie for their dear old Uncle Toby.

On the way home the knee almost decided to stop peddling gas, so I detoured slightly to County Hospital and groaned into the emergency room, past the numb row of urban walking wounded to a woman in white inside a window-frame reception area. Only her head was showing. She was simply short but looked decapitated.

"I want to see Doctor Parry," I told the disembodied head with its shock of stiff red hair. "He's my nephew."

"He is no longer at County," she said. I hoped her hands would come up to get rid of the headless image, but they didn't. "Joined the Army."

Parry was not my nephew. He was a young resident whom I had attached myself to as my personal medic. I felt depressed as hell and in real need of that hot bath and Bob Hope.

"If you'll have a seat," said the head, "someone else can take care of you."

I looked around and estimated the wait before I received medical attention as four weeks to a decade. I could have bullied and tricked my way in, but I was too depressed.

"What is your emergency?" tried the head flatly.

"Mortality," I said, dragging my foot behind me toward the door like the Universal Mummy.

Back at the boarding house, I pulled myself up the stairs trying to avoid Mrs. Plaut, who caught me before I made it to the top. She was as close to deaf as a human can be and still function, but she had heard me clumping.

"You had a call, Mr. Peelers," she said. "Don't remember who it was. I think he said Charlie McCarthy. Couldn't be." Her almost-eighty-year-old frame turned away. "And there's no hot water. I forgot to pay the gas bill again. I'll take care of it first thing Monday."

"Thanks," I said, completing my journey up the fourteen stairs, clutching my Walgreen's bag to my bosom.

Gunther came into the hall and looked with some concern at my leg.

"Phil," I explained.

Gunther had encountered Phil before and needed no further explanation.

"No hot water," he said.

"I know," I said back.

"I'll boil some on your hot plate," he volunteered and disappeared into my room. I followed him, threw my coat on the one semicomfortable chair in the room, and took off my clothes. Gunther went back to his room for a huge pot. I stripped to my underwear and watched him struggle with the pot that weighed about as much as he did, but I didn't offer to help. Pride should be respected.

I made it to the bathroom, found it unoccupied, and went inside. I brushed my teeth and let some cold water into the tub.

I got through a few lines of the Hope book: "There was a great excitement at the little house next door to the Barretts of Wimpole Street. My best friend was having a baby. Me."

That was as far as I got. Gunther, like a diminutive Gunga Din, lugged the boiling water in and dumped it into the tub. I climbed in and let out a groan. Gunther climbed up on the toilet seat and waited patiently.

"You wish company or not?" he asked.

I explained the Faulkner case and asked Gunther to try to track down someone at Bernstein's Fish Grotto who might have seen or remembered Faulkner or Shatzkin and find out whether Shatzkin had made a reservation the day he met Faulkner. I would try for Mrs. Shatzkin and Vernoff the writer. I also had some guilt pangs about Lugosi and again considered picking up Dave and Nate later in the afternoon and taking them to the show where I could spend a few minutes with Billings.

"Life gets ted-jus, don't it," I said.

"That is an idiom?" Gunther said seriously, perched upon the toilet seat.

"Line from a song by a guy named Bert Williams," I said, pulling myself out of the tub. "And now to work."

CHAPTER FOUR

With Gunther's help, I got my knee bandaged tightly. With a couple of pain pills Shelly Minck had given me months earlier for my back, I was ready to work, provided I didn't have to run and no one kicked me in the kneecap. I made some phone calls. I got the home address of Jerry Vernoff, the writer who had worked with Faulkner the night before, from the telephone directory. Using Martin Leib's name got me Shatzkin's home address in Bel Air from Warner Brothers. Shatzkin's office was listed in the phone book.

A call to Vernoff told him who I was and told me he would be home to see me in a few hours. A call to Shatzkin's office let me know that his secretary was there helping the junior members of the firm keep their world in order. Her name was Miss Summerland, and she wearily expected to be in the office for many hours. I didn't call Mrs. Shatzkin. She might not want to see me. I simply got in my pigeon-egg-green car and headed for Bel Air, admiring the frost on the few people in the streets. Even Westwood was nearly empty of UCLA students.

Bel Air is as exclusive as you can get and still be within

bragging distance of the movie studios. It has its own police and its own privacy. I talked my way past the guard at the entrance by telling him I was from the funeral parlor handling "things" for the Shatzkin family. He was properly professional and sympathetic, which means he made it clear he didn't much care. My car made him a bit suspicious, but I told him it was a loaner while my Rolls was being repaired. The story was idiotic, but the business card I handed him reading "Simon Jennings, Brentwood Funeral Services" was real enough. I had a whole stack of assorted cards given to me as payment by a job printer whose sister-in-law had stolen his 1932 Ford.

I found the house on Chalon Road, a big two-story brick building set back in a wooded area on a hill. It was impressive. A chauffeur was washing a real Rolls in the open garage and trying not to freeze. I knocked at the door, and it was opened almost immediately by a Mexican girl in black who looked so somber that I wasn't sure whether to believe her.

"Peters," I said seriously, opening my wallet to show her my identification and knowing she wouldn't take a close look. "I'm investigating the crime. I'd like to talk to Mrs. Shatzkin."

The maid stood back, I moved forward, and she said she'd get Mrs. Shatzkin.

I held my hat in my hand and kept my coat on, looking as serious and official as I could. I examined the hall mirror with suspicion and continued to do so when I heard the footsteps behind me and saw Camile Shatzkin in the mirror. I turned to face her.

"Officer?" she started. She was a good-looking woman, dark, dressed in black, with her hair worn up in one of those complicated hairdos. She was a little plump, but certainly not little. She reminded me in some ways of my former wife Anne, but in some ways she didn't. Camile Shatzkin's furrowed brow and wringing hands complete with handkerchief evoked Kay Francis in a melodrama, and Kay Francis was always up to something.

"Peters," I said and then before she could think of questions, "Officer Cawelti talked to you, but a few things have come up since last night that I need confirmation on."

"I'm not sure . . ." she began, looking back into the house for someone who didn't come. "It's been a very . . . horrible . . . I'm sure you understand."

"Fully," I said sympathetically, "but this will only take a few minutes.

"Very well," she said with a pained smile, but she didn't offer to guide me to another room or a seat. We talked in the Mexican decorated hall. I pulled out my new Walgreen's notebook and pretended to read questions.

"Who invited Mr. Faulkner here last night?" I began.

"My husband," she replied, turning her eyes to the floor.

I pretended to write and nodded in approval.

"How did you know the man who came here last night was Mr. Faulkner?" I said as sympathetically as I could. "You've never met the man."

"Well, yes," she said a bit nervously, "but I have seen his picture on book jackets and in the newspapers, and Jacques did tell me he was coming. I recognized him as soon as he came through the door. I . . ."

She was ready to break down so I came to her rescue.

"I understand, Mrs. Shatzkin. We have to be sure. Can you identify this picture as Mr. Faulkner?" I pulled out my wallet, reached in, and withdrew a small photograph that I handed to her.

"That's the man," she said with a sob, handing the photograph back to me.

"You're sure?" I said, taking it and putting it back.

"I'll never forget that face," she said, covering her eyes.

Well, that was a step toward Faulkner's defense. The photo she identified was one of Harry James that had come with the wallet when I bought it at the dime store. I decided to push Mrs. Shatzkin a bit.

"We'll need a photograph of Mr. Shatzkin," I said, putting my notebook away.

"There are no photographs of Jacques," she said sadly. "I wish to God there were. He wasn't fond of being photographed."

"Everyone has a photograph of himself somewhere," I said. "Especially a man as prominent as Jacques Shatzkin."

Suspicion flared in Camile Shatzkin's eyes.

"Do you have a photograph and some identification, Mr. Peters?" she said. "I'd like to make sure you are not a reporter trying to get a story at the expense of my grief."

"The only photograph I have of myself is when I was ten," I said, reaching for my wallet and knowing I had no identification that would please her.

"Well, perhaps we can find a photograph of Jacques when he was ten," she said. The widow's grief had given way to determination. Kay Francis was running the company and she meant business. "Your identification."

I pulled out my private investigator's card and showed it to her.

"You said you were a police officer," she hissed through even, white teeth.

"No, I didn't," I said. "You and your maid simply assumed I was. I'm working for Mr. Faulkner's lawyer and . . ."

"Haliburton," she shouted, her breast rising like a coloratura's.

An enormous figure in a black sweater, wearing as granite a face as could be carved, hurried into the hall from the rear of the house. He looked at Camile Shatzkin and at me, waiting for her orders.

"Now wait," I said, holding up my hands and knowing I had no chance of making a run for it on my former leg. "We have a legal right to question witnesses. We could have done this through the district attorney's office, but . . ."

"Haliburton," she said firmly and left the room.

Haliburton had clearly spent his life lifting cars and putting them neatly on shelves. He advanced on me without emotion and with very little sound.

"Haliburton," I said, "I know when I've had it. I'm leaving."

His hand caught the back of my neck and spun me toward the door. Without thinking, I threw my left elbow back in the general direction of his face about half a foot up in the air. I caught him in the windpipe, and he let me go. I scrambled for the door, pulling my leg behind me without looking back. What I did was meant to be a run but probably looked like a Fourth of July handicap race. I heard the door open behind me as I made it to the car. The chauffeur stopped, wiped his hands, and watched from the garage as I opened my door and locked it just before Haliburton grabbed the handle. He was clearly angry.

"No hard feelings," I said, putting the car in gear as he tried to put his fist through the roof. I could see the dent he made. I backed down the roadway fast, extinguishing a couple of well-trimmed shrubs. Haliburton must have been the gardener because my attack on the shrubs brought out the worst in him. He came thundering down the driveway, picking up a rock as he ran. On Chalon Road I straightened out and managed to avoid hitting him as I pulled away. The rock hit the hood, scratched its way along, and flew up the windshield, taking off into the air toward Uranus. I headed out of Bel Air, watching the receding dark figure of Haliburton in my rearview mirror.

Another day, another friendship formed. Dale Carnegie could have hired me cheap as a negative example. But I had learned something. Maybe.

Although she might come up with a more firm identification later, as of now Camile Shatzkin, who had identified William Faulkner as the murderer of her husband, couldn't tell Faulkner from a trumpet player. I hummed "You Made Me

Love You" to keep from thinking about my knee and headed for Sunset Boulevard and Jacques Shatzkin's office.

The Jacques Shatzkin Agency was on the second floor of a two-story building on Sunset not too far from Bel Air. The first floor of the building housed some elegant stores—a women's dress shop on one side and The Hollow Bean, an import shop, on the other. The flight of wooden steps was varnished and clean. There were twenty-two steps and each one sent an accordion of pain through my bandaged leg. The trick would be to avoid stairs and keep my leg straight.

The reception area inside the heavy wooden door was clean, bright, and comfortable. It was easily as big as Shelly's office and mine combined, with room to spare for Union Station. There was no receptionist, but I could hear voices to the left through an open door. I now had a good sense of the decor of Jacques Shatzkin's offices: elegant, homey. Carpets, thick and dark; chairs, low and soft. The desks were old and highly polished; the walls a light brown. Fluorescent lights twinkled overhead. It reminded me of a funeral parlor, except for the pictures on the wall of clients and near-clients and friends of the deceased. "To a good man—Frank Fay," "For my friend Jacques—Edward Everett Horton," "I don't see anything funny about it—Robert Benchley," "To a guy who can be trusted—Preston Foster."

"And they meant it," a voice cut through my reading. I turned to a willow reed of a woman, a dry woman in her fifties with short brown hair and a brave smile on her face. She wasn't beautiful and she wasn't homely. She was simply a face in the crowd, but her efficiency was evident in her straight back, neat blue suit, and hands folded in front of her.

"Miss Summerland?" I said.

"Mrs. Summerland," she corrected. "Those photographs are not just for show, Mr. Peters. . . . You are Mr. Peters?"

"I am," I confessed.

"Mr. Shatzkin was a very likable man," she said with affection and a too-rigid control.

"I won't take much of your time," I said.

"That's all right," she said, stepping back from the doorway in which she was standing. "Please come into my office. Some of the other members of the agency are in the conference room worrying about the future. I'd rather cling to the past for at least a few days more."

I walked past her into the office, which was small and decorated in the same homey manner as the reception area. She went behind the desk but didn't sit. I got off my leg and into the chair, knowing I would have to look up to and at her for the conversation. I could see she would be more comfortable that way and I didn't want to make the mistake I had made with Mrs. Shatzkin.

"The police think William Faulkner killed Mr. Shatzkin," I said.

"I know," she returned flatly.

"I represent Mr. Faulkner. He says he didn't do it. Had no reason to do it. Hardly knew Mr. Shatzkin." I shut up and looked at her, waiting for a reply.

"As far as I know," she said, "and as I told the police officer earlier, they met only once for lunch."

I eased out my notebook and began writing.

"Did they get along at that meeting?" I asked.

"I wouldn't know," she said. "I wasn't there, and they did not come to the office, at least Mr. Faulkner didn't. He simply called, asked to talk to Mr. Shatzkin, and the two of them arranged it. It's right on Mr. Shatzkin's calendar, if you'd like to see it. One o'clock lunch with W. Faulkner on Thursday."

"I believe you," I said. "Do you know where they ate?"

"No," she said.

"Did Shatzkin particularly like Bernstein's Fish Grotto?"

She looked puzzled and shook her head.

"He never mentioned it. I doubt that he would go there for lunch unless Mr. Faulkner insisted. It's too far away, and Mr. Shatzkin was not particularly fond of seafood."

"Couple more questions and I'll be done," I said with a

smile. "Do you know what they were supposed to talk about at the luncheon?"

"Mr. Peters, why do you not simply ask Mr. Faulkner?"

"Because," I said, "some things are not making sense in this. I'm not quite sure what they are, but something is cock-eyed besides my old science teacher at Glendale High School."

"I don't know what Mr. Faulkner wanted to talk about, but I think it had something to do with getting Mr. Shatzkin to represent him."

"Okay," I said, standing up. "Do you have any photographs of Mr. Shatzkin, by any chance?"

"No," she said emphatically. "There was one on his desk, but Mrs. Shatzkin sent her handyman Haliburton to get his things, including the wedding photograph on his desk."

There was a lot in the way she said it that made me go on. She had underlined both *Mrs.* and *her handyman*. There was also the suggestion that the widow could have waited until the corpse had cooled before spring cleaning.

"Mrs. Shatzkin identified William Faulkner as the man who shot her husband," I said.

Mrs. Summerland shrugged.

"I think she was lying or mistaken," I continued.

"Both are possible," said Mrs. Summerland, looking me straight in the eye. "But what isn't possible is that Mr. Shatzkin lied, dying or not. If he said Faulkner shot him, then he told the truth. Mr. Shatzkin was a quiet, honest man. He wasn't the fast-talking pitchman who some . . ." Mrs. Summerland's composed exterior was about to shatter into tears, and she didn't want that, at least not in front of me.

"You've been very helpful," I said, closing her door behind me just as her head went down.

The sun was almost out when I limped outside, and it was a little warmer but not warm enough to resell my coat to Hy O'Brien. Things were starting to pile up, and the heap they formed might mean something, especially if I got it burning.

My next stop was the apartment of Jerry Vernoff off La Brea in Inglewood. It was a one-story courtyard job with a small pool in the middle and some stunted yearning palms cutting off the sun. I knocked on his door and knew from my experience in such places that everyone who was home heard the knock vibrating through his walls.

"Yeah," came a voice.

"Peters," I said.

"Right," said the voice. I waited a few seconds, and the door came open on a slightly soft but reasonably good-looking big guy with straight blond hair and a smile. His teeth were white. His skin was tan and his shirt was open.

"Come on in," he said. "Find a place to sit. I've got to clean my hands. Messed up a can of chili."

He disappeared, and I looked for a place to sit. There was a sofa and two chairs. There was also a card table set up as a desk with a chair. On each of these pieces of furniture there were piles of paper and index cards full of writing.

"Just pick up a pile and shift it," he shouted. "But try to keep it in order."

I opted for one of the chairs. I moved two piles of typed notes onto the floor and sat down.

"Can I get you a drink?" Vernoff shouted over running water. "A beer or a Coke?"

"Coke is fine," I said.

He came back with a bottle for me and one for himself.

"I can't even cook a can of chili," he said with a grin.

"I know the feeling."

"Shoot," he said, draining a third of his Coke.

"You work with Faulkner?" I said.

"Well, I do on this job. I'm a free-lance story man," he explained. "See all this," he said with a sweep of his left hand to take in the pages and the wall of books. "Cabinet in the corner is filled with plot cards. I've got hundreds of them. Hell, I've got thousands. If you count the possibilities for mixing and matching, I probably have a million plots in this room. Producers and writers hire me to get them going, give them a start, some ideas. I shoot plots and variations at them to see if they can get something going in their imaginations. The pay is reasonably good. The work has been pretty steady for the last few years."

"And you like it?"

He shrugged and gulped down another third of the bottle before he grinned in my direction.

"It's all right until I can sell one of my own screenplays. Hey, about Friday, I told the cops Faulkner and I were in his hotel room."

"But you said he went out around nine."

"Right," said Vernoff, "but that was to throw down a few drinks. Faulkner has been known to tie one on from time to time. That's what did him in the last time he worked out here."

"Why didn't you go with him?"

Vernoff laughed, and I made a dent in my Coke.

"He didn't invite me. Our Mr. Faulkner is a rather private man, and to tell the truth I don't think he liked working with me. I move too fast, think too fast. I made him nervous, but hell, that's what I was getting paid to do, to stimulate him, get him moving and thinking."

"You like him?" I asked.

"Not much," he admitted, "do you?"

"I don't think so," I admitted. "But I don't think he killed Shatzkin."

"I don't even know he knew Shatzkin," sighed Vernoff. "Shatzkin's my agent, or was. Can't say he did a hell of a lot of good for me, but he was a good man. The whole thing doesn't make sense. I'm not even going to do a plot card on it."

"Maybe you can work out a plot to tell me who killed Shatzkin and why," I said, finishing my Coke and standing up.

"Sure," he said, joining me. "I could think of a lot of them. It's all there." He pointed at the file cabinet. "Numbered and ready if you know what to look for. Say, it's lunch time. You want to share a can of chili and a hunk of lettuce?"

I agreed, and we moved into his kitchen, which was an extension of his living room, full of papers, newspaper clippings, books, and notes. He cleared two places at the table and served the chili in two bowls directly from a messy pot that I could see was burned at the bottom. Vernoff told me about his adventures with various writers, including a stint with F. Scott Fitzgerald, who had come to the apartment, looked at the mess, and departed on a one-week binge. In turn, I told Vernoff about some of my more celebrated cases, concluding with the Bela Lugosi problem.

"I've got about two hundred cards on vampire plot variations," he said dripping chili on a copy of *American Mercury*. "I could do a vampire script in five days . . . no, three days, but nobody wants vampire scripts. They want war stories. That's what I was trying to feed Faulkner, but he kept getting melancholy about the war and some brother who died in an airplane. Say, I earned my money working with him."

I finished up, we shook hands, and he asked whether he could get in touch with me some time to work up some plot cards from my cases. I told him it was fine with me and left him to clean up the dishes and find the typewriter he had temporarily misplaced.

I headed home because it was easier to park there than my office, and I wanted to catch Gunther. I passed Mrs. Plaut on the way in and said, "Good afternoon."

She smiled back and said with as much relevance as was her wont, "You didn't bother yourself."

Gunther was in his room, which looked like the model for a *Good Housekeeping* ad. Everything was always in place and clean. His books on the shelf were all lined up evenly, and there was seldom more than a book or two on his desk and a manuscript.

"Well, Gunther," I said. "How did it go?"

He took out his notebook and read:

"Shatzkin made no reservation nor did Faulkner when they ate at Bernstein's. If they were there, they simply took their chances. No one recognized them or remembers them. Both lobster *naturale* and the shrimp salad are, of course, on the menu."

He put the notebook away and looked at me. After borrowing a couple of nickels from Gunther, I went down the hall to the pay phone and got through to the Wilshire station. I asked for my brother.

"Pevsner," he growled.

"Brother of Pevsner, Son of Pevsner. Grandson of Pevsner," I answered.

"What the hell do you want? Hold it." Then, to someone in his office, "So don't book him. Just take him upstairs and question him a little before you let him go. . . . Okay, Toby, what do you want?"

"Listen," I said, "I've got some questions on the Shatzkin murder you guys may want to follow up."

"Take it up with Cawelti," he said.

"Can you just listen?" I shouted. "You've got me hobbling around this damn city. The least you can do is listen."

"Talk fast," he said. Age or war scare was creeping up on Phil. He actually responded to an emotional plea. I didn't like it.

"I saw Mrs. Shatzkin. She's pretending to be broken up, but she's not. She never saw Faulkner in her . . ."

"Besides the time he came through the door and shot her husband," Phil put in.

"But how did she know it was Faulkner? When I showed her a picture of Harry James, she swore it was Faulkner."

"She's a confused woman with a lot on her mind," Phil said impatiently.

"She's a confused woman who has devoted some of her first morning of widow's grief to getting rid of photographs of her husband. Now why would she do that?"

"She doesn't want to be reminded of her grief," he said. "Is this all you've got?"

"Why did Shatzkin take Faulkner to Sixth Street to eat? It's nowhere near his office, and he didn't like seafood. It looks like he wanted to go somewhere where he wouldn't be recognized."

"It looks that way to you," said Phil. "To a jury and me it looks like he went to Bernstein's. What has this got to do with anything?"

"Faulkner says Shatzkin called him to set up the meeting," I went on. "Shatzkin's secretary says it was Faulkner's idea."

"We didn't book Faulkner for a lapse of memory or for lying about his business deals," Phil returned to his growl.

"Okay," I gave it another try. "Faulkner says Shatzkin was a loud-mouthed, fast-talking pusher at lunch. Shatzkin's secretary says the dead man was a pussycat."

"So where are you taking this?" Phil demanded. "We've still got the dead man's statement. I've got it right here." I heard him shuffle some papers and then read. "Officer Bowles: 'Take it easy, sir.' Shatzkin: 'Faulkner shot me. William Faulkner. Why did he do that?' Officer Bowles: 'Take it easy, Mr. Shatzkin.' Mrs. Shatzkin: 'Officer, it was Faulkner. He came right in and shot Jacques for no reason, no reason.' We also found the gun in Faulkner's hotel room."

"Someone's trying to frame him," I said.

"A unique argument," rasped Phil.

"And no motive," I said.

"Take your tale to Dick Tracy," he said and hung up the phone.

I invested another nickel and called Vernoff.

"I forgot to ask you something," I said. "Why did Faulkner leave just before nine last night? Why not earlier or later? Just coincidence?"

"I don't remember," said Vernoff. "I think he just said he needed a break and would be back in an hour."

"Thanks," I said and hung up. I needed another talk with

Faulkner, and I owed Bela Lugosi a day's work. A few more of
Shelly's pain pills got me back to the station. This time I was
led down to the lock-up where Faulkner was sitting in a cell.

"Mr. Leib believes there is a chance bail can be set for me
in spite of the charge," he said, putting aside the book he was
reading. The turnkey hovered impatiently at my side.

"This'll take a second or two," I said. "I need some answers. Whose idea was it to eat at Bernstein's?"

"I told you it was Shatzkin's," he said impatiently.

"Why didn't you go up to Shatzkin's office?"

"Because he was walking down the stairs when I arrived.
He recognized me and we simply turned around and walked
out. I fail to see the relevance of these questions."

"I'm not sure I do either," I said. And it was clear that the
fat blue-uniformed turnkey didn't see the point.

"Shatzkin called you to set up the meeting."

"That is right."

"On Friday night when you were working with Vernoff,
whose idea was it to take a break just before nine?"

"I think it was mine. I found the man barely tolerable and
had quite as much as I could absorb. Working with him was not
my idea but a condition of the studio. He actually told me that
he could reduce *As I Lay Dying* to one hundred fifty plot cards.
The man is a menace to creativity."

I bid Faulkner goodbye, resisted the temptation to chuck
the turnkey under his five chins, and limped outside with the
feeling that I had something in all this, but I didn't know what
the hell I had.

CHAPTER FIVE

On the way back to Hollywood, I stopped at a fifteen-minute car wash, watched some guys in blue overalls fail to turn my speckled Buick into a pumpkin, paid my forty-nine cents and decided to stick with the Faulkner case. I'd give Lugosi a rebate or something for each day I didn't work. I needed the money, but there wasn't much of me to go around and what there was was fragile.

I was heading up Van Ness when I spotted my tail, a dark Ford two-door about a block behind. The sky had clouded fast and promised rain to give my car an extra wash it could now do without. The sudden darkness made it tough to see who was driving the Ford. I turned right on Santa Monica and then left on Western, moving slowly. Sure enough, the Ford appeared a block behind, taking cover behind a Rainer Beer truck. I went down on Fountain and made a circle around the block, turning on two wheels and hoping no patriot had spotted me burning rubber. U.S. Rubber was running full-page ads in magazines and the papers telling us that for the duration of the war "every ounce of rubber is a sacred trust." I even had a copy of their free thirty-two-page booklet, "Four Vital Spots," on how to make tires last longer, but I considered this a potential emergency. Arnie, my no-necked mechanic on Eleventh, could get me retreads if things got bad.

With my right fender rattling enough to frighten an old man walking his dog, I made it around the block in about ten seconds. Figuring the speed my tail was going, I should have wound up right behind him, but I didn't. He was gone. I prowled the neighborhood for a few minutes and headed home to the boarding house on Heliotrope.

Assuming the dark Ford was not a ghost out of my past, and that was not an entirely reasonable assumption, then the likelihood was that it had something to do with the Faulkner case. Somewhere in this busy Saturday, I had touched a nerve. But why follow me? To see where I was going? Whom I was talking to? Probably. At this point, it wasn't likely that I was on a potential victims list, but you never knew. When I parked a block away from the boarding house, I took my .38 from the glove compartment, convinced myself that it still worked, pocketed it, and got out. The rain caught me ten feet from the car. It was a cold rain that poked through my coat and made it heavy. My knee told me not to run so I plodded along, abandoning renewed plans for an assault on Carmen that night.

When I got to the porch, I looked like an enormous sponge. Mrs. Plaut was there, beaming down as I lumbered up the stairs and leaned against the wall.

"They bring May flowers " she said brightly.

"It's January," I said, "not April."

I shed my coat to ease my burden up the stairs.

"You had another call, Mr. Peelers."

"Charlie McCarthy again?" I asked.

"No, Baylah Lougoshe," she said precisely, pronouncing it correctly. "She had a very strange accent."

"He, Mrs. P.," I corrected, "it's a man."

"I think she was Norwegian," she guessed.

"Do Norwegians have different accents from Swedes?" I said before I could stop myself.

"Definitely Norwegian," she said, turning to smile out at the rain.

The stairs were lonely, high, and steep, but I had promises to keep, so up I went, coat in hand, heart in mouth, brain in gear.

I fished Lugosi's home phone number out of my sopping wallet and called on the hall phone. A child answered.

"Is Mister Lugosi there?" I asked.

"Hello," he repeated brightly.

"Is he there?" I tried. "Or anyone more than three feet tall?"

"He's working a movie. He's a doctor."

Someone took the phone away from the boy.

"Hello," I shouted.

"Mr. Peters," came a woman's voice.

"Right," I said.

"Mister Lugosi is at the studio, Monogram, shooting. He wanted to know if you could meet him there. He said it was rather important."

"What was it about?" I asked, taking off my wet jacket and watching the trickling trail from my clothes creep down the stairs behind me.

"He didn't say," the woman said. Her voice was pleasant, efficient, and strong, and she was ignoring the boy in the background demanding something that sounded like "Skpupsh." She told me where Monogram was, but I didn't need the information. I needed another bath and a large towel. I thanked her, hung up, and made it to my room, where I left a trail of discarded wet clothes on the way to my mattress on the floor. Two days earlier I had been thinking of picking up a few dollars by pumping gas. Now I was floating in clients and water.

Ten minutes later, I forced myself up, rebandaged my leg,

gulped a few more of Shelly's pain pills, and put on my second suit, which was too light for the weather and too dirty for society. I tried not to think about the rain that was telling my bad back to beware. Maybe I succeeded. Maybe my old theory that the body can tolerate only one major pain at a time was true. Come to think of it, it wasn't my theory. I got it on a Shadow radio show from a mad scientist who was torturing a girl he wanted to turn into a gorilla. I'd have to tell Phil my pain theory the next time he tried to hit me with a desk.

And still I waited, looking out at the falling rain, knowing I had a block to go to my car, knowing my coat would be of no use. A large bowl of Grape Nuts mixed with puffed rice and too much sugar helped. I felt better, but wasn't thinking any better. The rain looked as if it was stopping or at least taking a dinner break. Giving myself a pep talk about responsibility and financial security, I braved the elements, scanning the street for the dark Ford. There were a few parked on the street, but they had been there when I came in. Almost all the cars in the world were a solid dark color, except mine. A lot of those cars were Fords.

I stopped for some gas at a station downtown on North Broadway and drove past the Los Angeles River viaduct. I remembered from somewhere in high school history back in Glendale that this had once been the center of an Indian village, home of the Gabrielino Indians. They had been a branch of the great Uto-Aztecan family, which spread across North America from Idaho south to Central America. At one time twenty-eight Indian villages existed in what was now Los Angeles County.

The Indians, according to what I had been told, were among the most peaceful in North America. They seldom warred. Robbery was unknown, and murder and incest were punishable by death. They believed in one deity, Qua-o-ar, whose name never passed their lips except during important ceremonies, and then only in a whisper. The men seldom wore clothes and the women wore only deerskins around their waists. When the weather got rough, the Indians wrapped themselves in sea otter fur. Their homes were woven mats that looked like beehives. They had no agriculture, and they didn't know how to domesticate animals. They lived on roots, acorns, wild sage, and berries and—when they could catch them—snakes, rodents, and grasshoppers. Their weapons were sticks and clubs. They didn't know how to make bows. Los Angeles had come a long way in a few hundred years.

Monogram in 1942 was a thriving, catch-as-catch-can operation with some studio space, but not much, and a lot of shooting in the park to save a few dollars. There was no big, fancy gate and regiment of uniformed guards, but they did their best to keep up appearances. An old guy in a gray jacket and cap, who looked as if he had been riding horses for a century, hurried out to my car when I pulled up.

"Yeah?" he said.

"Right," I came back. "I'm here to see Bela Lugosi. I'm doing a job for him."

"Peters?"

"Right."

"He said you might be coming. I thought he might be pulling my leg. He's got one screwy sense of what's funny sometimes." The old guy waved me in and put his hands on his hips. He smiled after me. There wasn't any need to tell me where to find Lugosi. The place wasn't that big. I just followed the sounds past low buildings to a sound stage about half the size of anything at Warner Brothers. In a space marked for Sam Katzman, I parked behind a truck with a rusting rear door and moved as quickly as I could on my aching leg to the entrance. My attempt at speed was prompted by a desire to keep warm without a coat and not by any particular zeal for the job at hand.

The light over the door was off, indicating that no shooting was going on. Two guys, one Oriental, the other huge, were talking in front of the door about the Chicago Bears-Pro All-Stars game the next day. The Oriental guy was saying something about Sammy Baugh when I went through the door.

The stage was well lighted. The set in front of me was a phony jungle with a little hut. Three guys were huddled around a camera and from their anxiety I guessed they were having trouble with it. Lugosi, wearing a dark suit and thick makeup, was seated on a crate outside the range of lights smoking his cigar. He spotted me, stood up, and advanced on me into the shadows away from the others.

"Ah, Mr. Peters, good of you to come," he said. "I could not reach you, and I did not want to leave a message at home for reasons you will no doubt understand."

He was nervous and it was affecting his accent, which became more pronounced. *Doubt* had come out "dutt," but there was no trouble understanding his concern.

"Before I left for the studio this morning," he said, removing his cigar, "I got a phone call, a man, a voice I did not know, with an accent, if you will believe, stronger than my own. This man said, 'We are going to get you now. You have only days to live.' Then he said I knew who he was."

"Either we have a new player," I said, "which isn't likely, or our friend has gone another step and changed his pattern: a direct threat on the telephone."

"Shall I call the police, ask for protection?" he asked.

"You can try, but I don't think you'd get it, and the police can't watch you forever. I can't even do that. The trick is to find our friend as fast as possible. I'll get on it."

"Thank you," Lugosi said seriously, pumping my hand.

"Ready in a few minutes, Bela," a voice came from the group gathered around the camera. Lugosi waved to the men to let them know he was ready, and a young woman with a script in her hand ran to the stage door and called in the two men outside.

"Excuse me," Lugosi said. "We have to work quickly.

Time is money. I am the most expensive part of this film and it is a modest expense."

I walked with him toward the set while the Oriental who had mentioned Sammy Baugh moved in front of the lights, waiting for Lugosi.

"What's the picture?" I asked.

Lugosi shook his head and smiled sadly.

"A very timely epic written last week and not yet finished. It's called *The Black Dragon*. I play a plastic surgeon who transforms Japanese into Occidentals so they can spy on America. In the end, I am to receive ironic justice for this misdeed. It goes on. I look in the mirror in the morning and I say to myself, 'Can it be that you once played Cyrano and Romeo?' Always it is the same. When a film company is in the red, they come to me and say, 'Okay, so we make a horror film.' And so that is what we do, what I always do. And I do my best. That is the trick." He adjusted his tie, took a last puff on his cigar. "Always play it seriously no matter what the material. And always talk slowly so you will have more screen time."

Lugosi stood erect, convinced his face into an evil smile, and stepped into the lights.

"I'll be in touch as soon as I have anything," I said. He nodded in acknowledgment. "And I'll have someone watching your home just in case."

With this he turned, dropped the film smile, and gave me a real one, which I returned. Then a voice shouted, "Quiet on the set," and I went out the door.

I found a taco place, sat in a corner near a window where I could watch the dark Ford that had picked me up again, and thought about things. I thought that I was eating too much and always did when I was on a job. With two jobs I was eating even more. I thought that the guy in the dark car might not be from the Faulkner case. There was a good chance that he was Lugosi's pen pal. I thought that Los Angeles was a strange place to work and that people here found the strangest way to die. I thought of Billie Ritchie, the Charlie Chaplin imitator, who had died of internal injuries after being attacked by ostriches while making a movie. I thought until the thinking hurt as much as my knee, and I knew I was ready. I was ready for one more Pepsi and a final taco before I played another round of tag with the Ford.

It was just about dark when I lost him. He was easy to lose because he didn't want to get too close. I made some plans for getting a good look at him the next day if he kept up the game. It might be the best lead I had in one of my cases.

Back home I avoided Mrs. Plaut and borrowed a handful of nickels from Gunther. The next day was Sunday. Gunther volunteered to drive up to Bel Air and keep an eye on Camile Shatzkin, follow her if she left. I didn't expect much to happen, but at least I'd be on the job through Gunther. Gunther's car was a '38 Oldsmobile with a built-up seat and special elongated pedals put on by Arnie the garageman for a reasonable price. The car was inconspicuous enough, but a midget was not the ideal person for a tailing job. I had no choice. I called my poetic office landlord, Jeremy Butler, and asked him to spend Sunday keeping an eye on the Lugosi house just in case the threat was real. Butler heard my story and said he would park discreetly with a book and keep an eye on the house. A near giant is no less conspicuous than a midget, but as I said, my options were limited, and as a bodyguard Jeremy Butler had no peers. I couldn't say the same for his poetry. My last set of nickels went for a phone call to North Hollywood, where my sister-in-law Ruth answered the phone.

"Ruth, Toby. Hey, I thought I'd take the boys to a show to see *Dumbo* tomorrow if they're not doing anything."

"I'm sure they'd love it, Toby. What time will you pick them up?"

"About noon. I'll take them for lunch first."

"I'll have them ready," she said and hung up.

Below me the weekly Saturday night roomers' poker game

was starting, presided over by Mrs. Plaut with a retired post-man as the perennial big winner. I had sat in once and likened the experience to Alice's at the tea party. My knee was feeling a little better. I turned off the lights, got into bed, and listened to the reborn rain on the roof and my radio. I caught the guy on the news saying, "General Douglas MacArthur's Philippine defenders are carrying on a grim and gallant battle against tremendous odds on the island fortress of Corregidor at the entrance of Manila Bay. They have successfully driven off the third bombing attack on the island."

The Chinese high command reported that 52,000 Japanese had fallen, but the Japanese had taken Changsha. The Russians were still giving the Nazis hell, but the British were taking losses 280 miles from Singapore.

I turned off the radio and went to sleep, wondering whether there were some place on the earth not at war. I had a trio of dreams. One took place in Cincinnati. A vampire was flying through the streets dropping little pellets. Anyone who touched one or was touched by one turned to stone. The second dream had something to do with airplanes in a small room, and the third dream struck me as brilliant, something I'd have to remember in the morning so I could tell Jerry Vernoff the next time I saw him, if ever. It would make a perfect plot card. It involved a murder in a locked room. The victim was blud-geoned to death but there was no weapon. Just the victim and the murderer. In the dream I figured out that the killer, who looked something like my brother Phil, had frozen a huge ba-nana, used it as a weapon, and then eaten it peel and all. The victim looked something like me.

When I woke up, I reached for my pants and notebook to write down the dream and then thought better of it. It didn't seem so clever on a Sunday morning with the light through the windows and a layer of fuzz on my tongue.

My knee was stiff but not terribly painful as long as I didn't bend it. I dressed and ate a big bowl of Kix while I read the Sunday funnies in the *Times*. I skipped the news. Red Ryder and Little Beaver had returned to Painted Valley. A "Sinister Sheik" was about to slash Tarzan. Dixie Dugan was trying to get her father out of his easy chair, and Fritzie Ritz and Phil were taking a walk. Joe Palooka was in the Army, and Tiny Tim was getting thrown into a Mason jar by Hoppy. The comic book insert—Brenda Starr, Kit Cabot, Spooky, and Texas Slim—inside the funnies kept me busy through another bowl of Kix.

By the time I got to my brother's small house on Bluebelle in North Hollywood it was almost noon. The baby was toddling around the living room with a padlock in her hand and a four-toothed grin for me. Nate and Dave came out ready to go. Nate was twelve and Dave nine. I tried not to compare them to me and Phil. Dave had just recovered from a car accident, which had added to the Pevsner financial burden.

"Did you kill anybody yesterday, Uncle Toby?" Dave asked brightly.

"You're a zertz," Nate broke in. "He doesn't kill people every day. He hardly ever kills people."

"I hardly ever kill people," I agreed.

I picked up the baby, who hit me with the small but heavy padlock and grinned. I was grinning back when Ruth came in the room, looking like Ruth: skinny, tired, with tinted blonde hair that wouldn't stay up and a gentle smile. I took a step forward and saw Phil at the kitchen table with his head in the funnies trying to avoid me.

"What happened to your leg, Toby?" Ruth said, with some concern.

"Shot," said Dave. "Probably Nazis."

"Nazis," I agreed, loud enough to be sure Phil heard. "They attacked me when I wasn't looking for putting my feet on their secret spy desk."

Ruth shook her head, thinking I was making a fool joke

and being willing to tolerate me. I handed Ruth the baby, who gave me a final blow with the padlock, and I promised to have the boys back by five.

"Give my best to Phil," I said as we went out the door.

"Your car is nifty-looking," Dave said.

"Thanks," I said, letting them in. When we were on our way, I cleared my throat and said, "You want to see *Dumbo* or some scary movies?"

"Scary movies," the boys said in unison.

"Right," I agreed, "but you have to tell your mother and father you saw *Dumbo*. It's part of a case I'm on. Okay?"

They agreed, and I headed for Sam Billings's adobe theater. We ate at the taco place across the street, and Nate complained about a sore stomach while we waited in line. The line consisted mainly of kids of all sizes with a few adults and a hell of a lot of noise. When we got to the box office, I asked the girl where I could find Billings, and she said he had an emergency dental appointment.

"Boys," I said. "Here's a quarter for candy. Watch two of the movies and meet me out on the sidewalk in front of the theater when they're over. What movies are you going to see?"

"*Revolt of the Zombies*," grinned Dave.

"*Dumbo*," overrode Nate wisely.

I made it to the Farraday Building in fifteen minutes and took the elevator up because of my leg. That took another ten minutes. The building echoed empty on a Sunday morning, and I knew not even Jeremy Butler roamed the halls. He was watching the Lugosi house and probably worrying about someone defacing the sacred walls around me.

Billings was, indeed, cringing in the chair with Shelly hovering over him when I entered.

"Toby?" Shelly said, turning his glasses in my direction.

"Right," I said. Billings looked in my direction. His eyes showed recognition.

"Got the book I was telling you about," Shelly went on cleaning a silver mirror by blowing on it before inserting it in Billings's mouth.

"Right over there. *Civil Air Defense* by Lieutenant Colonel A. M. Prentiss. Every type of bomb and every means of defense."

"Terrific," I said, moving closer. "How's Mr. Billings's mouth?"

"Emergency," Shelly said in a whisper that not only Billings but also anyone in the corridor could hear. "Lots of work. Bad situation. Never saw anything quite like it. Wears false fangs. Throws his bite off. Can you imagine?"

"Yes," I said. "I'm the one who sent him to you, remember?"

"Right," Shelly agreed, searching for his stub of a cigar somewhere among the magazines and instruments.

"Can I ask Mr. Billings a few questions? Quick ones?" I said, deferring to Shelly's professional position.

"Ask, ask," Shelly sang in delight while he continued his search.

"Mr. Billings, I need your help," I said. Billings tried to sit up, but the chair was tilted, and Shelly reached out to push him firmly back. He didn't want this one to escape.

"Mr. Billings," I said, leaning close. "I need the names and addresses of all the members of the Dark Knights of Transylvania. I need the real names and real addresses, and I need them fast."

"Mr. Peters," he said with a determined protest, "that can't be done. The Dark Knights of Transylvania isn't a club, it is a sacred commitment. Our membership consists only of those who believe in vampires and who are determined that the image of vampirism be respected. The world has always been full of those who do not want to know the truth. We must remain secret until the world is ready to accept the truth."

"This is an emergency," I said, moving my face close to his and showing my clenched teeth.

Billings looked determined, so I went on before he made it too difficult to give in, which I wasn't going to let happen even if I had to torture the names out of him, which I didn't think would be difficult or necessary.

"Mr. Billings," I said. "Someone has been trying to frighten Bela Lugosi, and I have reason to believe it is one of your Dark Knights. Yesterday Lugosi got a phone call threatening his life. This is a serious business."

Billings's eyes had gone wide and his face pale when I mentioned the phone call. I wasn't sure what there was about that part of my story that got to him, but it did.

"I don't understand," he sputtered.

"I don't either, but I'm going to find out. Now you either give me the names and addresses out of concern for the good name of your organization, a sense of decency, and concern for Lugosi, or I smash your nose into a duplicate of mine."

"And he could do it," Shelly agreed over his shoulder, continuing to hum a tune.

Billings gave me the names and addresses, and I wrote them in my notebook.

"Thanks," I said, patting him on the shoulder. "Shelly will give you his preferred patients discount, won't you, Shel?"

"Right," agreed Shelly, anxious to get to work on Billings's distorted mouth. "The usual. I'll definitely get an article out of this. A nut whose mouth has been distorted by vampire fangs. I'll call it the vampire syndrome, a first in dentistry."

"Has a nice ring," I said, heading for the door. "You're in good hands, Mr. Billings."

Billings's pudgy hand rose in response to my goodbye wave, and I headed for the door. Before I got there, Shelly told me I had a call from Jerry Vernoff. I went back to my office and called him.

He answered after almost a dozen rings.

"Vernoff," he said in a deep businesslike voice I didn't recognize.

"Peters," I said.

"Oh," he answered, his voice returning to normal. "I thought it was Zugsmith, the producer. I hear he has a spy serial he needs plot work on. I have a call in to him. I've been clipping newspaper articles on spies for the last year, a diamond mine of plots, enough to keep five series going." His voice was filled with excitement.

"Sounds terrific," I said. "You called me?"

"Right," he said. "I thought I'd try to help on the Faulkner business. If I hadn't driven him up the wall he wouldn't have gone out the door, and either he'd have an alibi or he wouldn't have done Shatzkin in."

"I prefer the alibi option," I said.

"I tried to find a bartender who remembered seeing him," Vernoff said. "No luck. Tried for a housemaid or something in the hotel, but nothing doing. There's an elevator operator who thinks he saw Faulkner around nine, but he can't be sure. I'll keep at him, and maybe he'll get more sure unless you want to talk to him."

"No," I said, testing my knee to be sure I was able to move with some show of normal animal ability. "You keep at it." It didn't sound like much of a lead. Even if the elevator operator started to grow more sure, he'd be cut down in a trial if it ever came to one.

"Great plot material," Vernoff said. "Hey, I don't want to be morbid or anything, but a man can't help thinking professionally. You know what I mean?"

I knew what he meant. Most people had long since stopped being people to me. They were potential victims or victimizers. That's all there was in the world except for the bedazzled and bemused semiguilty who wandered through life.

The world wasn't a place with a few dark corners, but a place with countless numbers of places to hide.

"I know," I said. "Give me a call if you find anything. I appreciate any help I can get, and I'll let Faulkner know."

"Right," he said. "And if you come up with anything, I'd really appreciate talking. I can't help feeling a little guilty about what happened to Faulkner."

"I know," I said.

"I better get off the phone now," Vernoff laughed. "Zugsmith may be trying to get through."

I hung up so Vernoff could spend a few minutes or hours or forever waiting for that call. Vernoff had probably spent years of his life waiting for that phone to ring so he could pitch plots.

CHAPTER SIX

The list was short with no phone numbers and no home addresses, only businesses:

Bedelia Sue Frye, Personality Plus Beauty School, in Tarzana.

Wilson Wong, New Moon Cantonese Restaurant, on Seventh Street in Los Angeles.

Simon Derrida, The Red Herring, in Glendale.

Clinton Hill, Hill and Haley Contractors, Beverly Hills.

It was a pretty broad geographical and social spread. Since it was Sunday, there was a good chance I'd catch none of them at work. On the other hand, I had three and a half hours before I picked up Nate and Dave. Wilson Wong was the closest and, since restaurants are open on Sunday, the most likely to be at his address. The sun had warmed up the day and my disposition. Doing my Alan Ladd act on Billings had also done wonders for my ego. It's not everyone who can threaten a short, fat, helpless would-be vampire in a dental chair.

The New Moon had its own parking lot, with eight cars in it. The restaurant itself had a wooden façade painted red and designed in late Charlie Chan. The inside was dark and filled with whispering customers having a late lunch.

A skinny Chinese guy with a small, polite smile came up to me.

"How many in your party?" he said.

"None," I answered, trying to look tough. The image of Alan Ladd was still with me. "I want to see Wilson Wong. Business. Private."

"Certainly," said the waiter, who motioned me to follow and made his way between tables. I followed him to a door down a corridor past the men's and women's rooms. He knocked and paused.

"You like football?" said the waiter while we waited and he knocked again.

I told him I did.

"That's a trouble living in California," he confided. "No good pro football. You think the Bears will clobber the All-Stars?"

"No," I said, "with Baugh at quarterback, the Bears will be lucky to win."

"Maybe so," he said doubtfully as the door opened to reveal Wilson Wong, who wore a dark business suit and tie and a surprised look.

The two men exchanged words in Chinese and Wong turned to me as the waiter left.

"Please come in, Mr. Peters," he said. "It is Peters, isn't it?"

"Right," I said as he closed the door behind us.

It was less an office than a library. Three walls were filled with books. If there was a window, it was covered by books. A firm reading chair stood in one corner with a light over it, and a desk stood off to the right with neat piles of notes. Wong offered me a chair and I sat down. He joined me, passing up the reading chair so we'd be at the same level of comfort or lack of it.

In the basement of the theater two nights earlier, Wilson Wong had appeared the energetic gadfly. In his office, he looked anything but.

"It was my belief that our real names were to be kept secret," he said, "but I am not surprised. Mr. Billings is not the most discreet of souls. Can I offer you some coffee, tea?"

"Tea," I said, thinking it appropriate for the setting.

Wong went to his telephone, pressed a button, and said something in Chinese. I assumed he was ordering tea or my assassination, depending on whether I had come to the right or wrong suspect. He settled himself back in his chair and looked at me with curiosity.

"Now," he said. "What can I do for you?"

"The easiest thing is for me to tell you the story and you to give me some answers," I said. He thought that would be fine so I got comfortable, meaning I let my sore leg hang free, and told him the Lugosi tale and my part in it. He listened, nodded, and paused only to answer the knock at his door and the delivery of tea on a dark tray. He put the tray on the desk and poured us both cups of tea.

"I'm afraid I can't help you greatly, Mr. Peters," he said. "Unless your visit convinces you to eliminate me from your list of suspects, thus simplifying your task."

"That's one way," I said. "Now can you convince me that you have no reason to give Lugosi a bad time?"

"Rather easily, I think," said Wong with a smile. "I have almost no interest at all in Mr. Lugosi If you look around at my shelves, you will discover two kinds of books in both English and Chinese. Many of my books are sociological in nature. Some are historical and quite a few are on the occult. Although this business is mine through inheritance and is one in which I take deep familial pride, my primary interest is in the exploration of social groups, cults if you will, that use the occult as a focal point. While I do not display it prominently as a matter of pride, I hold a Ph.D. degree in sociology from the University of Southern California and I do some teaching at the university. I have also written two books on the subject we have been discussing for the University of California Press."

"Then you have no real interest in . . ."

"No," he finished for me. "The group itself is somewhat interesting but I've gathered about as much from them as I care to, and I have been contemplating removing myself from their midst, though it is difficult, considering the small membership. One develops a certain affection and understanding."

"Los Angeles must be a pretty good area for your work," I said, draining my tea cup and getting a refill.

"It is, indeed," said Wong. "I think that is one of the reasons I concentrated on this specialization. I would be foolish to attempt to study the social life of the Eskimo with a base in Los Angeles."

"I see your point," I said. "Can you give me any suggestions or ideas about who might be the one in this group I'm looking for? What I know of vampires comes from some movies and reading *Dracula* when I was about twenty."

Wong got up and walked to his desk with a sigh, looking for something.

"Like so many of the lower-California groups," he said, "this one consists of individuals who are particularly ignorant of that in which they profess to be most interested, leading one to conclude that they are committed not to a belief in vampires and vampire lore but to role-playing and dressing-up. For example, no member of the Dark Knights is at all aware of the Aztec rituals that took place in this very area hundreds of years ago, rituals that are more closely allied to vampirism and its meaning than that of Dracula. The Aztecs regularly sacrificed young women and children and consumed their blood and bodies in the belief that this would prolong their own lives.

"The Chinese vampire," he continued, still searching for something on his desk, "is far more frightening than the Transylvanian vampire or Oupire. The body of the vampire in China is said to be covered with greenish white hair and to have long claws and glowing eyes. Chinese vampires can fly without turning into animals. To prevent a corpse from becoming a vampire, animals—particularly cats—must be kept away from the body, and the rays of the sun or moon must not touch it or the corpse may receive Yang Cor and be able to rise and prey on others."

"Fascinating," I said, shifting the weight on my leg.

"But you are interested in the group," he said, "and not in being a vampire historian. My assessment from past experience suggests that the short thin man with the New York accent is not a believer either—though, I confess, I do not know what he is trying to gain from the group. He is certainly no scholar. Ah, here it is."

Wong pulled out a sheet from a pile before him.

"I wrote some notes on the members and planned to do a bit of follow-up, but not really very much," he said. "Getting the names was no great problem, though I do not plan to use them in my writing. However, I thought some background on each might be useful. If you do gather such information that might be helpful and if it does not violate your ethical code, I would be glad to pay a research fee."

"I'll think about it," I said. "I'm not sure what my ethical code is on this thing. What about the woman?"

"Yes," said Wong, looking at his sheet. "Bedelia Sue Frye. In some ways a very interesting example, totally within the role, totally the vampire during the meetings, never a break or flaw, but the vampire she portrays is not one of historical significance or myth but one of movies. A definite possibility for you, Mr. Peters."

"Hill?" I said, referring to the tall guy who had said nothing.

"A voyeur, I would guess," said Wong. "Respectable by day. Likes to do something dangerous, but not too dangerous. He needs to have a secret. He is never comfortable engaging in any of the rather juvenile rituals, but he clearly gets satisfaction from watching. A possibility for you, Mr. Peters."

"And Billings," I said.

"A sad man unable to sustain his fantasy within his body and abilities. A sad man. But that is an observation from outside. I view his state as sad. I have difficulty knowing how he perceives his own state."

"Well, Mr. Wong," I said, getting up on my incredibly stiff leg. "You've been a big help."

He walked over and extended his hand.

"Then I take it I am no longer a suspect?" he said.

"You're still a suspect," I said. "The only way to get off my list is to become a victim, and I'll still be suspicious."

Wong laughed.

"Academic research lost a good man when you decided to become a detective," he said.

"I didn't decide," I said, following him to the door. "It just happened."

Wong walked at my side through the restaurant and out the front door.

"If I can be of further assistance," he said, "please feel free to return."

I thanked him and turned. The parking lot was not quite as full as it had been, and there was no one in sight when I reached my car door. The sky suddenly went dark or a shadow went over the sun. At least that was my impression. I looked up to see which it was. What I saw should have moved me into action, but it didn't. It simply froze me on the spot. On top of my Buick stood a caped figure in black. The sun was directly behind it so I could see no features. It leaped at me, swinging some object in its hand. My body finally reacted, dropped flat, and rolled away, taking only part of the blow from the object on my retreating head. The dark figure turned to try again, and I covered my face and head with my arm as I rolled away on the gravel parking lot.

"Nosferatu," came Wilson Wong's familiar voice, and the black-caped figure turned to face him. The guy in the cape swung his shiny club at the Chinese professor, who dropped to the ground and threw a well-timed kick at the back of the leg of our daylight vampire. The guy lost his balance and his club, righted himself before he hit the gravel, and ran out into the street with billowing cape.

"Are you all right Mr. Peters?" Wong said, sitting up, his suit a mess.

"I think so," I replied, joining him and touching my bleeding scalp. "Was that judo?"

"No," said Wong, helping me up. "I was on the wrestling team at USC. A simple leg drop. But the years have eluded me. I was lucky. We'd best get you to a doctor."

I touched my head, trying to assess the degree of damage from years of experience. Koko the Clown was perched on my shoulder, ready to take me into the inkwell if I passed out, but I silently told him he'd have to wait, that we'd play some other time.

"I think I'll be all right," I said. "I just need some water and a bandage and a place to clean up a little."

Wong led me back through the restaurant, past now-curious customers, and helped me clean up. The waiter gave us a hand and found some cloth for a bandage. A shot of something alcoholic offered by one of them sent a bolt through me, threatened nausea, and then gave me the power to move.

"Thanks," I said.

"Whoever that was, he lacked true style," Wong said.

"But he was effective," I added.

"Yes," said Wong. "It appears as if Mr. Lugosi *is* in some danger."

I made it back to my car without further problems, fished my .38 and holster out, and clutched them to my bosom. A sudden chill ran through me, and I turned quickly, thinking someone was breathing down my back from the rear seat. It was empty. I locked the doors and eased into the street, looking for dark Fords and darker strangers.

I made it back to the theater by 4:30. Nate was eating Jujubees and David was wiping tears from his eyes.

"Hi, kids, how was the show?"

"Great," said Nate, scrambling into the back seat.

"I got scared," said Dave, moving next to me, "and Nate the Great wouldn't take me out."

Nate reached over to hit his brother on the head.

"Cut it out," I said. "If you guys want to do this again with me, cut it out. Okay?"

"Okay," they agreed.

Dave wiped tears from his red face and looked at my bandaged head with curiosity.

"What happened to you?" he said.

"Nazis," I said. "I had to kill them."

"How many?" Dave said, with his mouth open.

"Thirty-one," I said.

"He's kidding you, dope," Nate said from the back seat, popping a handful of candy in his mouth and turning to watch a fire engine through the rear window.

I got them back home at five and Ruth greeted us at the door.

"Baby's taking a nap," she said. "I'm just starting dinner. How was *Dumbo?*"

"Terrific," said Nate. "It scared Dave."

"The part where the zombies . . ." he began, and I cut in.

"The part where Dumbo's mother dies," I said. "Right, Dave?"

Dave nodded glumly.

"What happened to you?" Ruth said, looking at me up close. My bandage was high on my head, and my final suit was only partly presentable after a roll in the gravel.

"Near riot at the show," I explained. "Kids trampled me in the rush for tickets."

"Trampled right on his head," Nate confirmed. "I saw it."

Ruth didn't know what to believe.

"Staying for dinner?" she asked. "Tuna on noodles."

"Phil home for dinner?" I asked.

"Yes," she said.

"I think I'll skip it," I said. "I've got some work to do."

I was almost to the car when I heard her say, "Toby, take care of yourself." There was real concern in her voice, and I turned to look at her, wondering whether she saw me the way Wilson Wong saw Sam Billings. It was depressing.

I should have headed home to nurse my aches and see whether there were messages from my midget and giant investigators, but Ruth's words had cut deep. My response, I knew, would be to push harder, to prove I could take care of myself and come out on top, which I was not at all sure I could prove.

My car and body knew where I was going without being told by my brain. The car took me from the valley down Laurel Canyon and headed toward Sherman Oaks and beyond to Tarzana. There was about as much chance that a beauty school would be open on Sunday night as there was that Japan would launch its attack on California in the morning. But I couldn't face going back to the boarding house. I would have tried my ex-wife Anne but didn't have the energy to talk my way into her apartment for a flash of sympathy and a firm goodbye, which would have been more discouraging than nothing at all. I found a parking space with no trouble and looked west to see the sun going down. Night would be here soon, and other peoples' vampires would rise. My vampire paid no attention to such fineries as tradition. His trade tool was a tire iron and a good surprise.

Personality Plus was on the second floor of an ordinary neighborhood office building. It was open. The reception area had a counter behind which were shelves of bottles of hair products—hair conditioner, shampoos, mostly green with bubbles in them. A cardboard ad for Breck shampoo was displayed prominently on the counter. The carpet was marine blue and green, long-wearing but with no depth. Large color photographs, some of them badly faded, featured what were meant to be the latest hairdos, but the quality of the pictures led me to believe that they were probably a few years old.

There was a lot of traffic, women sitting in chairs waiting, some of them with children. I walked to the counter, behind which stood a youngish man wearing barber white. Behind him in a room with a lot of talk sat various women with white gook in their hair or wet red nails held out in front of them to dry.

"Can I help you?" said the young dark man.

I had expected a little mincing or a fey wrist, but he gave none and was all business.

"Are you always busy like this on Sunday night?" I said.

"Many of our customers work in defense plants," he explained. "We keep special war hours. Sunday is one of our busiest days. We're open till ten. Can I help you?"

"Bedelia Sue Frye," I said. "I'd like to see her. It's important. Is she a student here?"

"Miss Frye is the director of the school," he said, looking beyond me to see how the customers were taking me. I looked as if I were in search of an emergency room instead of a beauty operator. On second thought, maybe I could use a little cosmetic help to put me in presentable condition.

"Terrific," I said. "Now can I see her? Tell her it's in connection with the Dark Knights. She'll see me."

"The dark nights?" he said incredulously.

"You've got it," I said. He left me to face the gathered waiting women and children. A few looked at me. Most kept their noses in their magazines.

The young dark man came back and asked me to follow him. I went around the counter and down a hallway, where we met a trio of white-clad young women, each carrying a human head in her hands. The young man didn't stop, and the women passed close enough for me to see that the heads were mannequins with hair done up in curlers. The deeper we went into the place, the stronger the smell, a sickly, almost sweet smell something like vinegar, but not quite.

"Through there," said my guide, pointing to a room. "Miss Frye will be with you in a minute."

I went through there and found myself in a white, bright office with a window showing out into a long room lined with chairs in which women were sitting having their scalps, hair, faces, and anatomies worked on, plastered, baked, and threatened by an ant colony of instructors and teachers. Even in the relatively thick-walled office I could make out the rumble of sound from the big room beyond. While I watched, a blonde woman in white strode down the aisle that separated the two rows of chairs. She was stopped every few feet by a student or customer with a question, a problem, or a crisis. Gradually, she made her way toward the room I was in. As she came closer, looking directly at me, I could see that she was somewhere in her thirties, built like Veronica Lake, and possessed of a white, gleaming smile that would have looked great in a Teal commercial. She opened the door, letting in the vibration of voices, and closed it again behind her.

"Yes, Mr. Peters?" she said.

"How did you know my name?" I said, leaning back against the small desk. "I didn't give it to Wilhelm."

"His name is Walter," she said, "and we met Friday. You wanted to talk to me?" She moved over to the desk, reached for a cigarette in a silver box, changed her mind, and looked at me with a smile and folded arms.

"I'm trying to stop," she said, crinkling her nose.

"You're Bedelia Sue Frye?" I said.

"I'm Bedelia Sue Frye," she said mockingly.

I looked at her for an incredible few seconds while her amusement grew. The height was right, but that was about it. This woman was a natural blonde with a healthy complexion and very little makeup. Her smile was as good as the sun, and she stood straight and was full of bouncing energy.

"The same one who's a member of the Dark Knights of Transylvania?" I said.

"The same," she said, holding up her right hand. "Honest. It's like a release for me. I dress up for the meetings, put on a wig, change my face, do a little acting. I'm under a lot of pressure here," she said with a shrug, "and at one time I had thoughts of going into movies. Actually got a few small roles and then I got into this." Her hand swept the room broadly and took in the outside. "None of my staff knows about the Dark Knights, and I was under the impression that no one would find out."

"I'm a private detective," I explained. "I was with Bela Lugosi Friday because he's had some threatening letters, phone calls, other things, and we have some good reasons to believe that one of the Dark Knights is responsible for the threats and that things may get worse."

"That accounts for the way you look?" she said, finally unable to resist the cigarette, which she took quickly.

"I think so," I said, reaching up to try my scalp.

"So," she said, "what can I do for you?" Her will power returned and she put down the cigarette.

"Putting it straight," I said, looking into her blue eyes, "I'm here to find out if you're the one who might be responsible for the threats on my client."

"Me?" she said, returning my look. "Why would I want to . . . that's ridiculous. I don't even believe in any of that stuff. And I don't care one way or the other about his movies. He looked to me like a tired old man. Anyone who would give him a hard time has to be an all-out looney, which I am not. Say, listen, I'd like to keep talking. I really would, but things are going crazy out there."

"Maybe we could get together some time," I said. "I mean get together and talk about the Dark Knights and Lugosi."

Her smile was broad and direct.

"That might be nice," she said. I reached into my pocket, got my wallet, and found my card. I grabbed a pencil from the desk and wrote my home address and the number of the phone in the hall of the boarding house. "I'll give you a call."

She took the card, looked at it, tapped it with her long

fingers, and tucked it in the clean pocket of her blouse over her heart. Things were never what they seemed, I thought, as she went back through the door and into the colony.

I made my way out, wondering what Wilson Wong would make of his prime suspect if he had been with me. I also realized that of the five members of the Dark Knights at least two claimed to have *no* commitment at all to vampirism. Back outside in the darkness, I made up my mind to wrap up both the Lugosi and the Faulkner cases as quickly as possible and investigate possibilities with Bedelia Sue Frye. I was not so twitterpatted, however, that I didn't watch my back and front as I went back to my car with my hand near my jacket and gun. I unlocked the car, checked the back seat, locked the door behind me, and headed home.

Home is where you go, and they have to take you in if you pay your rent and cause as little trouble as possible.

Back on Heliotrope, I found a message from Jeremy Butler saying the day had been uneventful, and I found an excited Gunther Wherthman, whose excitement waned when he saw me.

"I was attacked by a vampire," I said.

"Yes," said Gunther, following me into my room where I checked the corners and closet and locked the door behind us. "I too have something of singular import perhaps to report."

"Shoot," I said, moving to turn on my hot plate and searching for a can of pork and beans on my shelf. "Join me?" I said, holding up the can.

"No, thank you," said Gunther politely, brushing back a wisp of hair. "I have already eaten. May I . . ."

"Sorry, Gunther," I said, opening the can. "It's been a long hard lifetime."

"Mrs. Shatzkin went out twice today," he said. "Once she was driven by her chauffeur and went to the office of her husband. They remained in the office for no more than ten minutes. When they came out, the chauffeur was carrying a small cardboard box which seemed to contain odds and ends brimming over."

"Right," I said, finding a pot and filling it with pork and beans on the hot plate.

"It appeared to me to be of no singular import," said Gunther, "but I leave that to you. The second outing by Mrs. Shatzkin proved to be of greater potential interest, I think. Late in the afternoon she drove herself in a second car down various streets. I had the impression she was trying to see if someone was following her, but she was not very good at it. Her patterns of driving were most predictable and I let her drive around in recurring rectangles, picking her up at key points. It required some guessing, but my calculations proved to be correct."

"Good work, Gunther," I said, dropping a glob of butter into the boiling pot of beans.

"Toby," he said, "I was not giving my investigative mode to solicit approval, but to make clear that she did not know I followed."

"I'm sorry," I said, turning to him.

"Yes," said Gunther. "Well, she came finally to an apartment building in Culver City and entered. I followed after I was sure she was in and took down the names on all the boxes. There were six. By watching the windows from outside, I did manage to see her pass once or twice from the street side. The apartment was thus determined, and, I am sorry to say, it was the one with no name on the mailbox or bell. However, it was evident that she was not alone in the room. There was assuredly the figure of a man, and though I could not be certain, perhaps because my imagination was at this point engaged, I thought I saw what could at one point be interpreted as an amorous embrace. She remained inside for almost one hour and fifty minutes, emerged, looked around, and drove directly back to her home in Bel Air."

"The plot sickens," I said, moving to the table and eating directly from the pot with a large spoon and three slices of bread.

"And?" he said.

"I'll investigate in the morning. Gunther, thanks."

"I found it stimulating," he said. "Please call upon me if you need further help."

I told him I would and he left. After finishing my dinner, I checked my wet suit. It was drying reasonably well and might be ready by morning.

It was a little after eight on my Beech-Nut clock. While I got out of my clothes, I listened to the end of "Inner Sanctum." In bed, I heard Jack Benny and flexed my knee. It was working with some reluctance. I forced myself to exercise—push-ups, sit-ups, and panting. The knee would keep me out of the YMCA for a while, and I needed exercise as much to convince myself that I had an able body as to use that body.

I mixed myself a glass of milk with Horlicks, gulped it down, brushed my teeth, and got into bed with the lights out. I thought I'd rest for an hour or two, plan out the next day, Monday, and then get up and read a mystery. The rest turned to sleep, and I went out firmly except for one roll to my left that sent an icicle into my head wound.

The sound at the door was a scratch, and I couldn't tell whether the door was in my dream and the scratch outside or the reverse or neither. I struggled toward wakefulness, but it was one of those times when the weary flesh didn't want to respond to the need. I came out of it and sat up groggily. The scratch was still at my door.

"Just a second," I said, turning on the light and checking the clock. It was just after midnight. Gunther was probably suffering from his chronic insomnia and checking to see whether I was up for some talk or coffee, but I didn't take any chances. I got my gun and said, "Who is it?"

"Me, Bedelia," came the whispered answer. The voice was different from the one I had heard hours earlier in the Personality Plus Beauty School. I turned off the light, thought about putting on something besides my shorts, and decided there was no time. I stood to the side of the door with my gun ready and pushed it open into the room. From the light in the hall I could see the female figure silhouetted clearly. She was unarmed.

She stepped into the room, and I flicked on the light and closed the door. This wasn't the Bedelia Sue Frye I had met in Tarzana. This was the woman of the Dark Knights of Transylvania, the dark-haired, pale-faced creature slouching slightly, her voice a whisper, her smile a secret, a weary secret. She looked at my gun and let her eyes scan my body with a combination of amusement and approval. She was wearing something made of a red silklike material that hung straight down over her shoulders.

"You wanted to see me?" she said.

"Game time?" I said, looking closely at her. I couldn't be sure that this was the same woman, but it had to be.

"This is no game," she said seriously, moving to my one semicomfortable chair and looking at the room.

I put my .38 on a corner of the table opposite her, where I could get to it first if I had to, and scratched my head, being careful to avoid my bump.

"Look," I said, "things are going from bad to strange with me, and it'd make my life easier if you'd come out of character and tell me what's up."

"Up," she said with a smile, looking at my underpants. "You are."

I was. I sat down at my kitchen table and crossed my legs.

"Okay," I sighed, trapped in my own castle. "What's going on?"

"You wanted to see me," she said.

"I saw you this evening," I said.

"That was not the real me you saw," she said, looking at my mattress. "This is."

"Terrific," I said. "You really mean this, don't you? Or are you going to suddenly come out of it and start laughing when my pants come down."

"You can be amusing," she said, rising and taking a step toward me.

"Like a fly amuses a spider," I said.

"Perhaps," she said, with a pout.

My eyes went to the gun and back to her as she advanced on me. I didn't want to stand up, but I didn't know what was on her mind.

"Lady," I said, "I think you are a little screwy."

She sat on the table, a cat smile on her lips, and touched my face. I looked at her and wondered whether I was having a nightmare or a fantasy. She inched forward off the table like a cat and sat in my lap. My body told me she wasn't a fantasy.

"It is after midnight," she whispered, "when the blood runs free, and passion rises with the full moon."

"I don't know what's making the passion rise," I answered, "and I don't care. I'm not going to look a gift vampire in the mouth."

She took a small nip at my neck, but not enough to draw blood. I hoped she was teasing. Actually, I didn't know what the hell she was doing. My body told me to find out later. I tried to pick her up to carry her to my mattress-bed on the floor but my sore knee wouldn't take the weight. Must everything turn into a bad joke with me, I thought, and an echo answered fraud. I rolled her on the floor and time went for a long walk.

When we got up half an hour later, her black wig was still in place and she put her red silk dress on slowly while I sat on the mattress. I considered the fact that she was now closer to the gun than I was and decided that if I was going to be shot it might as well be like this.

"Do you come out of it now?" I said.

"There is nothing to come out of," she purred.

"Are you the one sending dead bats to Bela Lugosi?" I said.

She looked at me with a smirk. It was a comely smirk.

"He is old and tired and forgotten," she said. "It is the present that intrigues me. It is fresh blood. Like you."

"Thanks," I said, hoping she hadn't drawn blood from me without my knowing it. I resisted the temptation to examine my body. "I know where I've seen you before," I said. "You look just like the vampire girl in *Mark of the Vampire.*"

She smiled knowingly, moving to the comfortable chair.

"You know the one," I said, watching her face. "The one where Lugosi and the girl turn out to be fake vampires."

A sharp look crossed her face, and she stood pointing her finger at me.

"You have been given much and yet you mock," she said, walking to the door.

"Shall we make it same time next Halloween?" I said, still trying to shake her out of character, but it was no go.

"Perhaps we will meet again," she said and went out the door.

I got up and followed her to be sure she was gone. She was. I had been truly vamped, seduced, and abandoned by a wacko of the first order. It had been great fun, but it was just one of those things. I didn't think I'd be calling Bedelia Sue Frye for further talks unless I had some reason to think she was my harasser instead of the neighborhood schizophrenic.

I put a chair under the doorknob, left the light on, and went back to bed with my gun at my side. The year was young, and I had two more Dark Knights to visit. I wanted to be alive to visit them.

CHAPTER SEVEN

M y suit was dry by morning, or at least dry enough to
put on after I ate a large blue bowl of Wheaties and
listened to the 8:30 news. I wasn't sure whether we
were winning the war, but the Chicago Bears had beaten the
Pro All-Stars 35 to 24. An announcer told me Forest Lawn was
celebrating its silver anniversary as a memorial park. Founded
on 55 acres in 1917, he said, it had grown to 303 acres in
twenty-five years. I didn't see what they were so proud of. Mortality and westward migration were responsible. Then I found
out that John S. Bugosi, head of the FBI in Detroit, had ar-
rested a thirty-one-year-old stenographer in a local railroad
ticket office for "engaging in spreading vicious propaganda."

The sun was out, and the temperature was up to almost 50.
The bruise on my head had turned tender and purple. My knee
was stiff. It didn't hurt if I left it alone, but I couldn't bend it. I
decided to visit an orthopedic surgeon I played handball with
at the Y in the hope of instant, magical treatment before I went
to Culver City for a look-see at the mysterious apartment vis-
ited by Camile Shatzkin. The ride to Doc Hodgdon's office on

DeLongpre was uneventful: no dark Ford, no vampirelike creatures leaping on my hood. I kept my leg straight and respected its refusal to function. The radio crackled, but I listened to Our Gal Sunday tell someone named Peter about Lord Henry's escape from a fire.

Doc Hodgdon's office was in his two-story frame house in a residential area. Until a week ago I had thought he was a proctologist. Now I was glad he wasn't. I had no trouble parking. Walking, however, was another issue. I tried dragging my leg, hopping, and ignoring it. Hopping worked best, but looked silliest.

There were only three stone steps up, which I managed with circuslike dexterity, a grab at Doc Hodgdon's shingle with his name on it, and the help of two women who caught me as I was about to tumble backward down the steps. They looked like a mother-daughter set, with the daughter around fifty and both built like Broderick Crawford. They caught me under the arms and carried me through the door and alcove to the desk of Hodgdon's white-uniformed nurse receptionist, a twig of a creature with a mouth that a medium-sieve pea could barely enter whole.

The Brod Crawford ladies deposited me firmly and lumbered out like professional movers, leaving me to grab the desk to keep from falling.

"You have an appointment with doctor?"

"No," I said. "I'm an emergency."

"You need an appointment," the nurse whistled.

"If I let go of this desk, I'll topple over like King Kong," I explained reasonably.

She frowned and looked at the two patients who were waiting in what had once been a living room but was now an amber, many-chaired repository for Los Angeles's walking wounded. One patient was a chunky woman who had her face plunged into *Life* magazine. There was a heavy brace on her leg. The other patient was a fifteen-year-old boy with a burr of wild, uncombed brown hair on his head and his left arm in a heavy cast.

"You really have to have an appointment, sir," the nurse repeated stubbornly.

"Would tears move you? Just tell the doctor it's Toby Peters, foretopman, and it's an emergency," I said.

She got up reluctantly with both hands on the desk. Her plan may have been to demonstrate some massive hidden reserve of power gleaned from the Rosicrucians and whip the desk out from under me. She seemed to be considering this for a few seconds, then headed toward a door across the amber room. The fifteen-year-old looked at me with hostility.

"I got hit in the knee," I explained.

He nodded.

"It really hurts," I said.

He showed no sympathy.

"My shoulder's broke. Three places," he upped me. "Pop truck hit me."

"My brother hit me," I said.

"My brother hit me," the kid said, "I'd crush his face and walk on it."

"We have different brothers."

"My brother hit me," the kid went on, enjoying the taste of fantasy, "I'd rip both his ears off and shove them."

Doc Hodgdon came through the door in time to save me from further inventions of the youthful would-be Vlad the Impaler. Hodgdon was over sixty and had a head of white hair and a tan face to go with his lean body. I had only seen him in a YMCA sweat shirt and shorts before. At the Y, where he beat me regularly at handball, he looked athletic. Here he looked distinguished, like the guy in the Bayer aspirin ads. He strode over to me and took my shoulder firmly, helping me to his office while the twig nurse stood back as if my sore leg were contagious or I were taboo.

"What happened?" Hodgdon said quietly and with professional concern.

"His brother hit him," the kid said with contempt, probably considering a new retaliation on his own brother for some future affront.

Hodgdon closed the door to his office behind us and helped me to the examining table. The office-examining room had once been a dining room: Now it held a desk, a table, a cabinet, and framed certificates on the wall. The curtained windows looked out on a well-mown lawn with a pair of lemon trees.

"Kid was right," I said, squirming to get comfortable on the table.

Hodgdon rolled up my pants leg, probed, and fiddled with my knee. I gritted my teeth.

"Well," he sighed, standing erect, "you'll never play the cello again."

I held my tongue.

"It's not so bad," he said. "It's sore and slightly out of joint. You slept on that sore knee when it was in a semilocked position." He demonstrated semilocked with his fingers intertwined. It looked like firmly locked to me.

"Should have X rays," he said, "and rest."

"I haven't got the time," I said. "Isn't there something you can do to keep me going for a few days? It's an emergency situation. Life and death."

Hodgdon turned and looked at me levelly.

"I can try to straighten it while it's sore," he said, "but it would be painful and require a bit of guesswork on my part without X rays. If it worked, I could give you a shot to kill the pain and a knee brace. I suggest . . ."

"Do it," I said.

"Okay," he said and came to the table. Over his shoulder on the wall was a photograph of Thomas Dewey, the governor of New York. I met Dewey's little eyes and tried not to watch

Hodgdon, who touched my knee again and took a grip over and under it. I knew his hands and arms were strong. They had sent little black handballs zipping past my head for three years. "Here we go."

I yelled in surprise. Tom Dewey took it better. Pain I had expected, but not torture. My eyes filled with tears. When they cleared, I could see Doc Hodgdon bending my knee.

"I think you're in luck," he said. He went to his cabinet, opened it, pulled out a huge hypodermic, and filled it with a clear liquid.

"Maybe I should give the knee a rest," I said as he advanced, checking the liquid with a little spray into the air.

"It's all over," he said, grabbing my thigh firmly. I met Dewey's eyes again. Hodgdon's fingers probed my kneecap, found a space and plunged the needle in. This time I bit my teeth.

"You should be feeling no pain and be able to walk in two or three minutes," he said, placing the spent hypo gently in the sink. He opened the lower section of his cabinet and came out with an elastic hinged brace. It took him about ten seconds to get it on my knee. "Come back and see me in a few days. As soon as you can, give that leg some rest. That's all it needs now. And you can forget about handball for a month or so. I'll send you a bill."

In three minutes I was walking through the office, past the chunky lady with the *Life,* the twig nurse, and the kid with the cast. I didn't look at them, but I was sure they were all shaking their heads in disapproval. I went out the door, down the steps, and to my car, amazed at how little my leg bothered me. I didn't think about it long. I was back on my way to Culver City and the secret rendezvous of Camile Shatzkin. That sounded like a good soap opera title, but I had no one to suggest it to.

The place I was looking for was just off Jefferson Boulevard, and the apartment I wanted was clearly marked by the lack of name. There was some mail in the box, but I couldn't see whom it was addressed to, probably "Occupant." I rang the bell and got no answer. Then I tried the bell marked "Leo Rouse, Superintendent." A nearby ring told me Leo Rouse's apartment was on the ground floor, and an opening door confirmed my brilliant observation.

Rouse was around sixty, with an enormous belly and an equal number of teeth and strands of hair, about six. He wore overalls and a flannel shirt and was gumming something ferociously.

"Mr. Rouse?" I asked through the closed inner glass door.

"Yeah?" he said.

"I'd like to speak to you." I opened my wallet and showed him a card. He opened the door but didn't stand back to let me in.

"Mr. Rouse, my name is Booth, Lorne Booth, California National Bank."

"Your card said you was Jennings from Blast-a-Bug Exterminators," he said suspiciously.

I laughed.

"Got that card this morning from Jennings. They're doing an estimate on an apartment complex I have an interest in out in Van Nuys."

Rouse cocked his head and kept chewing. I estimated six to twelve hours before he could get down, let alone digest, whatever carnivorous thing he was worrying into masticated submission.

"What I'm doing," I said quickly, "is checking the credit rating of two depositors who are taking out, or at least asking for, a small business loan. Both coincidentally reside right in this building."

"Who?" he said.

"Long on the first floor and whoever is in apartment 2G. My notes have the address and apartment, but Mrs. Ontiveros failed to type in the name. She's had a lot on her mind with her brother Sid going into the Army and . . ."

"What you want?" said Rouse.

"How long has Long lived in this building?"

"Three, four years. They got no money to invest. Can't even keep up with the rent."

"Good to know," I said. "Just the kind of information I need. Now about 2G. That's . . . ?"

"Mr. and Mrs. Offen," he supplied. "Don't know anything about them."

"How long they live here?" I asked with benign solemnity.

"Three months, but they don't live here. They rent the place. Hardly ever sleep here. Hardly ever show up."

"Doesn't sound like the Offens who applied for the loan," I said, puzzled. "Could you describe them?"

"She's little younger than you. Some might say pretty. I'd say hoity-toity. Never saw him. She pays the rent. They're right above me. Every once in a while I hear his voice and another guy."

"This worries me," I said, leaning against the wall and pushing my hat back. "I'll tell you the truth, Mr. Rouse. I can see you're a man who can be trusted with a confidence. I've tentatively approved this loan, and my career could be in serious trouble if I make a mistake. Bartkowski in mortgages is near retirement, and I have a shot at his desk. I'd really like to take a look at the Offens' assets, very quietly, discreetly . . . it would mean a lot to me." I pulled a five from my wallet, and then another. Rouse stopped chewing, went back in his apartment, and exchanged words with a shrill woman before returning. He had a ring of keys in his left hand and his right hand out, palm up. I crossed it with the two bills, and he led the way up the stairs. The hallway was dark and slightly musty, though the building seemed to be only about ten years old.

"Your apartments all come furnished?" I asked.

"Right," he said, inserting the right key into 2G. The door popped open, and he stepped in and stood in the center of the room. It was clear he had no intention of letting me go in there alone.

"All I need," I said, touching my chin, "is some evidence of financial stability. A checking account, paid bills."

Rouse didn't answer. The room was small and furnished in unmatching bits and ends. The carpet was dark green, and the room smelled of dust. I tried drawers, tables, and behind the pillows on the sofa. Nothing. I tried closets and found no clothes. I even tried the garbage. There wasn't any. The refrigerator held three beers and a bottle of wine. There was no telephone. The only thing that indicated anyone had been in the two small rooms was the fact that the bedding was put on haphazardly. Someone had slept in or used the bed.

I put on a very sad face, a face of utter dejection that signaled the end of nations and careers.

"Nothing," I sighed. Rouse did not respond. "This is very distressing. Mr. Rouse, I wonder if I could impose on you further? If you hear Mr. and Mrs. Offen come back at any hour of the day or night, please call the number I'm going to write on the back of this card. My gratitude will be five more dollars."

"Right," said Rouse.

Someone was coming up the dark stairs when we closed the door, but I paid no attention until the footsteps stopped somewhere below us, maybe five or six steps. I looked down into the dusty darkness at a thin figure. Rouse looked down too. The figure stared in our direction for a beat and then leaped noisily down the stairs three or four at a time. I considered running down to take a look, but the slamming of the door and my knee told me not to. The figure had a distinct resemblance to the guy who had attacked me in Wilson Wong's parking lot.

"Who was that?" I asked Rouse.

Rouse shrugged. "Didn't get a good look. Someone with a key, though, else he couldn't get in downstairs. I didn't hear any buzzers."

I couldn't find my banker's card so I left Rouse the exterminator's card with my office and home numbers written on the back. I told him to ask for my assistant, Mr. Peters, and give him the message.

I didn't know whether Rouse believed any of my story, and I don't think he cared. He did believe in five-dollar bills.

There are times in every man's life when he has to decide whether he is going to face the Green Knight, Grendel, or Trampas. Most of us decide we can do without the encounter. But when one is getting paid and . . . Hell, there are some things a man just can't walk around. I think Gary Cooper said that once. The thing I couldn't walk around was named Haliburton and I knew where I could find him, at the Shatzkin house in Bel Air. Now I would have been pleased as Aunt Minnie's cat with a ball of yarn never to see Haliburton, but I had to talk to Camile Shatzkin again.

A car kept up with me for a few blocks but stayed far back. I was imagining dark Fords everywhere. I didn't see it when I got to Bel Air, where the same guy was on the gate as before.

"Are you coming to Mr. Shatzkin's funeral?" I said before he could come up with a reasonable question about my reappearance.

" 'Fraid not," he said.

"Too bad," I sighed. "It will be beautiful." He looked like he was about to say something so I started slowly forward. "We plan something special in conjunction with the Forest Lawn Anniversary," I said with a wave.

His eyes stayed on my car as I drove slowly up the road toward Chalon. It was the car that blew my cover every time. It was hard enough to play a role without a decaying mess of a car with a third-rate paint job giving me away. I knew where I could get a 1937 Studebaker for about $300, if I could get $300. It would make my life easier, but as my ex-wife would say, if I really wanted an easy life I wouldn't be doing what I was doing.

I checked my gun and opened my jacket to be able to flash it or even reach it if necessary. From the point of view of a nearly middle-aged mess of a detective, it was necessary. I felt noble and stupid as hell at the same time.

The chauffeur wasn't in the garage. Before I parked the

car, Haliburton was outside, hurrying toward me, his white shirt billowing in the breeze, a look of vengeful joy in his red eyes. He was the five o'clock commuter train ignoring the closed gate. I got out quickly, acutely aware of the crunch of gravel under his flying feet. When he was ten feet away, I opened my jacket so he could see the .38. That slowed him, but he didn't stop. I lifted the gun out and cocked it. He stopped almost within touching distance. The run had been short, but he was panting with excitement.

"You're not going to shoot anyone," he said.

"Is that a question?"

He took a step forward and I fired a bullet between his legs. Since my intent had been to shoot a safe five feet to his left side, he didn't know how lucky he was to survive. He backed away a few feet, shaken badly enough not to notice that I was shaking too.

"Assault and attempted murder," he said.

"Hell," I said putting the gun away. "I've been lying with a straight face all my life. I didn't shoot at you. I don't even have a gun with me. I'm an ex-cop with a brother on the force. I'll lay three to one you've got some reason why the police won't take your word."

"I'll get you alone, without the gun, little man," he said, pointing at me with his right hand and using his left to push the long hair from his face.

"That won't be necessary," Mrs. Shatzkin said from the door. I turned toward her. Her widow's black was still with her, but the outfit was more clinging and less somber. By the fourth day after her husband's death, she would probably be wearing white with flowers. "I've called the police."

"I suggest you call them back and tell them it was a mistake," I said.

She had already started to close the door, but I blurted out quickly, "They might want to know about a little apartment Mrs. Offen rents in Culver City."

The door stopped closing and opened. Mrs. Shatzkin turned to me, the sun in her face. For the first time, she looked as if grief had touched her.

"Haliburton," she said, her voice almost cracking. "Call the police. Tell them it was a mistake, that I thought I heard a prowler but was wrong. Tell them anything."

Haliburton looked from her to me in stupid puzzlement.

"I can . . ." Haliburton began, facing at me with clenched teeth and fists.

"Mr.—" she started.

"Peters," I said.

"Mr. Peters is coming in briefly. And I think it would be best if you forgot your quarrel with him. I was angry Saturday and very upset."

"You want us to shake hands?" I asked her.

"There's no need for sarcasm, Mr. Peters," she said.

"Sorry about your teddy bear," I said to Haliburton, walking right past him toward the door. My back went tight, knowing he was behind me, but I kept walking. It was one of those times. The adrenalin was running, and a Dybbuk was driving me. I entered the house and followed Mrs. Shatzkin into a comfortable deep-brown living room with thick, soft carpeting that looked as if no human feet had touched it.

She sat in a single seat, indicated the couch across from her, and then folded her hands in her lap. The red of her fingernails caught a flash of sun from outside. She was composed again.

"Are you a blackmailer, Mr. Peters?" she asked, her chin going up to show her contempt for such things.

"No," I said, taking off my hat and putting it on my lap. "I'm what I claim to be, a private detective doing my best to find out who killed your husband and hoping it won't turn out to be my client."

"Mr. Faulkner killed Jacques," she said emphatically. "I was . . ."

My head had been nodding a steady no from the instant she began, and she stopped abruptly.

"Who do you share that apartment with over in Culver City?" I asked softly.

Her face flushed. Camile Shatzkin looked like a human being instead of a mannequin for an instant, but she went back into her act.

"That has nothing to do with Jacques's murder," she said. "He is an actor, Thayer Newcomb. He would have absolutely nothing to gain by Jacques's death. He knows I would never marry him and that I would despise him if he hurt Jacques. As it is, I never intend to see him again. All of this has made it clear to me how much I really loved Jacques."

Her head was down again, and a handkerchief had appeared from nowhere. She pulled herself together and came up for another try.

"Mr. Peters, in spite of these surroundings and Jacques' business . . ."

"And his insurance?" I continued.

". . . and his insurance," she agreed, "I am not really a wealthy woman. I doubt if there is even a total of $800,000 after taxes."

"You had that figure on the tip of your grief," I said.

She stood up in anger, looked at my calm, mashed face, and sat down again.

"Just for the sake of Jacques's reputation and—I must admit—my own, I would like to offer you a fee for your services to keep the information you have discovered private."

"How much of a fee?" I asked.

"Well, let's say $20,000," she said.

"Let's say $50,000," I said.

"Very well," she said. "I would need a written statement from you guaranteeing that you would seek no further fee on this matter."

My head was shaking again.

"No money," I said.

She went flush again and bit her red lower lip. "I could offer . . ."

"And no offers of flesh, either," I added. "I have no ambition," I explained. "Absolutely none. I don't want or need a lot of money. I have no dreams money can buy. What I always need is just a little more than I've got, not a lot more, and I'm not about to be bought for a few hundred dollars. It's a bind, but it keeps my reputation clean and my suits old."

"And when you go to that great Pinkerton agency in the sky, they may reward you by making you a night watchman on the gate of heaven," she spat.

"Or the gate of hell," I added. "I'd like that. As for you and me having a social life together, I can't see you warm and friendly and sitting next to me tonight at the Wild Red Berry and Yukon Jake wrestling matches at the Hollywood Legion. No, Mrs. Shatzkin, I'll just have to amble out of here with my curiosity about your friend and a little more faith in the innocence of William Faulkner."

"I'm sorry you feel that way, Mr. Peters," she said, rising. I joined her. "If you should change your mind, please feel free to call me. Am I to assume, however, that you plan to take your information about my private life to the police?"

"No," I said, heading for the door. "I think I'll just find Mr. Thayer Newcomb and have a chat. You wouldn't want to make my job easier and give me an address, would you?"

Her lips tightened and her breasts rose. She was Joan of Arc defending her voices, a noble figure.

I went outside without an escort, closing the door behind me. Haliburton was at the car. He had obviously stopped the cops, but he hadn't stopped his mind, what there was of it, from working.

"No trouble," I said, holding my jacket open.

"No trouble," he said meekly. "I . . . what did you mean about Culver City and . . . what did you mean?"

Haliburton was a hurt and jealous lap dog, waiting to be whipped or given an order. I wasn't going to do either.

"I can't talk much about it," I said, easing into my car. He held the door firmly so I couldn't close it. "It has something to do with a private transaction Mr. Shatzkin made." He let go of the door and I closed it, but I opened the window to add, "Haliburton, I'd suggest you pack up your suitcase and head out someplace clean if I thought you'd listen, but you won't listen. You can't. The Medusa has made you stone deaf."

"Medusa?"

"Skip it," I said, and drove away. Like the last time, I watched Haliburton dwindle in my rearview mirror, but this time he was a slumped and defeated monster. There was no vengeance in those shoulders, only confusion.

I found a phone and reached Martin Leib, who told me to keep after the Thayer Newcomb lead though he had no great faith in it. He also asked me to stop by and brief Faulkner, who would be having bail set late in the afternoon, which meant that keeping his arrest for murder quiet would become more difficult.

"Even with county cooperation," Leib said, "I doubt if we can keep this from the press for more than a day, possibly two at most. If so, William Faulkner will simply have to live with the publicity."

"And Warner Brothers?" I asked.

"They will have to consider their options," he said like a good lawyer.

"Meaning, old Billy Faulkner will be dumped."

"He is not a charity commitment for the studio," Leib reminded me and hung up.

Faulkner was looking out his cell window when I got to the lock-up. The turnkey said I couldn't go in. I reminded him I represented the accused's lawyer. The turnkey said he didn't care if I represented a rat's ass.

"A Snopes," Faulkner said with a dismissive glance at the turnkey.

"I've got a fair lead," I told Faulkner. "You know a guy named Thayer Newcomb?"

Faulkner touched his mustache with his thumb and thought for a few seconds before saying, "I'm afraid the name has no meaning to me."

"There's a chance," I said, "that he set you up or helped set you up."

"Why on earth would a stranger go through all this trouble to try to make it look as if I had murdered Shatzkin?" Faulkner asked.

"Beats me," I said.

"Let's hope it does not," he added. "I've been passing my time here working out my own mystery tale, which will be as orderly and logical as life is not, as orderly as a game of chess."

"Full of knights gambiting around," I said, remembering the days of dodging my brother more than half my lifetime ago.

"Yes," said Faulkner, "a knight's gambit. Do you see yourself as a knight, Mr. Peters?" he said with a look that might be sadness or sarcasm, a protected look.

"No," I said, "I see myself in the mirror as little as I can. What about you?"

"Ah," sighed Faulkner, "I see myself in a hotel room alone with several bottles of Old Crow, and then I see myself with a small group of friends sitting up all night on a small island back home in Sardis Reservoir, turning spits, basting beef and pork, and singing 'Water Boy.' "

From looking in mirrors, he had turned to looking into the wishful future.

"I'll work on it," I said, but Faulkner had already turned to head back to the window.

The turnkey led me out, complaining of his sore feet. I could have told him some tales of sore feet and knees, but he wouldn't have listened. He was a talker. I was a listener.

With a stack of nickels in hand, I found a pay phone in a bar and called Shatzkin's office. I got Mrs. Summerland and found that Thayer Newcomb was not a client. She had never heard the name. The information operator didn't help either. I tried the large talent agencies and got nowhere. I was down to the last of my once-large stack of nickels and looking over my shoulder to see whether someone was pressuring me for the phone, when I got lucky. The Panorama Talent Agency did handle Newcomb. I said I was his brother James, a priest, in for a few hours from Dallas. The woman gave me an address, the Augusta Hotel. I blessed her and hung up. There was no answer in his room at the Augusta.

My Faulkner leads were running low. I could try Newcomb later or camp in the hotel lobby till he got there. Meanwhile, I could do a little work for Lugosi. I drank a Ballantine beer at the bar and listened to Vic 'n' Sade with the bartender. It was a little before one, and business was slow at that hour. I asked whether he had anything to eat, and he said he could slice up some cheese and slap it on a few pieces of bread with some mustard. I told him it sounded great. When he brought it back, it looked awful and carried a clear thumb indentation, but tasted fine, and I let myself sink into the amber afternoon darkness of the bar and beer, sharing a moment of repose with Sade, Uncle Fletcher, and Rush.

My next stop was Clinton Hill, the contractor who doubled as a Dark Knight, he of the falling wig and voyeuristic inclination, as Wilson Wong had said. I found the contracting firm in Inglewood just where it belonged, but I didn't find Clinton Hill. His brother was the Hill in the firm title. My boy, according to the angelic-looking girl at the desk, was an assistant librarian at St. Bartholomew's College a few miles away. He picked up his mail at the contracting office and, according to the girl, often let people believe it was his business.

The library was a few blocks down in a surprisingly large old stone building. It was surprising because the college itself consisted of a total of five decaying stone buildings enclosed by a rusting spiked fence and a couple of dozen acres of grass that could use mowing.

I found a space and spotted a dark Ford slowing down a block ahead of me. I watched for a few seconds while he hesitated and drove on. I decided to start taking down the license number of every dark Ford I saw and then checking to see whether there were any match-ups to prove I was either observant, scared, or both.

The library was impressive, like a chapel from another country. The lobby was marble and dark wood and the huge cathedral-size room with stained glass windows beyond was heavy, somber, and solid. The stained glass windows showed saints in various stages of torture or anguish. Saint Bart was the star of the show, and arrows abounded. I turned my head downward to more worldly things in the almost empty mausoleum. A few students were seated at the massive tables with books in front of them. Behind the wooden counter, which formed a protective circle, stood a librarian, a dry, tall man in a lint-catching dark suit. He actually wore pince-nez glasses.

"Yes," he said as I advanced. He made it clear that I was a foreign presence.

"Chadwick," I said "Professor Irwin Chadwick, UCLA, anthropology. I was talking to one of your librarians, a Mr. Hill, recently about your collection of works on the occult. I was wondering if he might be here to give me some assistance."

The dry man let gastric reaction take place, which faintly resembled human response.

"Mr. Hill," he said, "is not actually a librarian. He does work in the library, restacking primarily. He does, however, have a genuine knowledge of and interest in the occult. If you wish to go into the stacks, I think you will find him reshelving on the second basement level, in the four hundreds."

"Thank you," I said, heading in the direction he had pointed.

"You are welcome, Dr. Chadwick," he responded.

Behind us both the main door opened, but I didn't turn to see who was coming in. I made my way down a narrow row of books on metal racks piled about seven feet high and found a spiral metal staircase going both up and down. I went down slowly, trying to clank as little as possible, At the first level down, light was provided by some naked overhead bulbs and a few dusty windows that were probably even with the ground. I looked down the rows of books in both directions and saw nothing. There was a remembered smell of crumbling paper about the place. I went down another level. The spiral staircase rattled a little at its bolts but held as it probably had for a generation.

At the second level down were a few more naked bulbs of low wattage but no windows. I went to the left and realized that the floor was made of metal grillwork. I looked up and saw the ceiling was the same grillwork. There was a hollow emptiness to the place I didn't like. A level below held more books, but it was even darker and there may have been a level below that. I thought I heard a sound above and turned to look up. My turn caused an echo of my footsteps. I touched my gun. I was getting addicted to it. A few more encounters and I'd surely whip it out and accidentally shoot myself.

"Mr. Hill," I whispered, hoarsely, moving deeper into the aisle between the stacks. I passed rows of books on each side, going back fifteen or twenty feet each. A few rows had lights on, but most had them off. Strings hung from each light, and to turn a light on, one had to grope in semidarkness halfway down the aisle.

I moved slowly, peering down each aisle of books, right and left, trying to penetrate the corners, keeping a look of confidence on my face in case someone was hidden in one of the recesses. Maybe he or it would think I could see him.

"Mr. Hill?" I repeated. I was almost at the solid wall at the end of the narrow corridor. I found another set of spiral stairs

up and down. I was considering whether to go up or down or
back when a rumbling sound came out of the darkness behind
me. It was moving quickly and noisily out of a black aisle of
oversized books. I reached for my gun and pulled it out, backing against the stairway.

"Stop," I shouted, and my voice echoed below and above
in shadows.

The sound stopped and I could make out a shape in the
murk.

"You were calling me?" it said.

"Hill?"

"Yes," he said, emerging into the light, pushing a book
cart ahead of him that rattled noisily on the metal grill floor. He
was the same man I had seen at the Dark Knights meeting,
without the black hair. He had some hair, but it wasn't enough
to try to save. He looked at my gun in clear terror. I put it away.

"I'm sorry," I said. "I've had a few scares in the past several days. You know who I am?"

A wave of bitterness crossed Hill's face.

"You were at the Dark Knights meeting Friday. You are
not a member. How did you find me?"

There was a sob in his voice.

"I . . ."

"I'll quit," he said, near hysteria. "Billings promised,
promised in blood not to disclose anyone's identity."

"Blood?" I said.

"Simulated human blood," he explained. I looked in-
credulous, I guess. "Chicken blood," he clarified.

"I'm a private detective," I said. "My name's Toby Peters.
I'll make it fast and easy, and I don't care if you quit the Dark
Knights or the Morning Tulips, but I want answers."

Hill tried to push his cart past me, but I kicked it back with
my good leg, trapping him in the narrow aisle he had come out
of.

"Someone is trying to scare Bela Lugosi, maybe do more

than scare him, and I'm damned sure it's one of the Dark Knights, and I think I've got the suspects narrowed down to two. And you, old bat, are one of them."

"No," cried Hill. "I'm not one of those people. I just go to watch. I could never do any . . . I couldn't do things. I just stand around and keep my mouth shut. I couldn't even touch the chicken blood for the ceremony. You can ask the Count."

"Billings."

"Yes," he cried. "I live here, in the library. I don't even go out except to get some food, pick up my mail, and go to the meetings. I wouldn't hurt anybody or anything. I'm a vegetarian."

"You're a vegetarian?"

"Yes," he said.

"What has that . . . Forget it." If he couldn't stand the sight of blood he sure as hell hadn't sent an impaled bat to Lugosi. I would check his story, but I had the feeling it would hold up, which left me with damn few members of the Dark Knights.

"I practically live on ice cream alone," he went on.

"Okay," I said. "Forget it. Forget I bothered you."

I started down the aisle, leaving him behind.

"Are you going to tell them?" he pleaded. "Tell them what I really do, who I am?"

"No," I shouted. "Forget it."

He went silent with a small shell of a sob, and I hurried toward the stairway I had come down, but something stopped me. I stood still. Some of the side aisles had lights on when I had come down earlier. Now all the lights were off. It could have been a mass fatigue of ancient bulbs or my imagination. I considered going back to the far stairwell, but that meant dealing with Hill again. I couldn't face his complete breakdown. I pulled out my gun and inched forward very slowly and very quietly, but I still made some noise. I could see no one moving above or below and could hear nothing behind.

I made it almost to the stairway, convincing myself that

fear does strange things. Then fear appeared. It was almost noiseless and caught me in a near-dreamlike instant. It was a sound behind me, a movement of air. I turned in time to see the outline of a black-caped figure swooping down in a crouch from one of the stacks. I tripped backward, landing on my rear, and raised my gun. The black figure kicked, catching me on the wrist, and the gun spun upward out of my hand, hitting a bookshelf and going off. The bullet parted the distance between the black figure's face and mine and made him pause before he could deliver another kick. I could hear the gun drop to the steel floor below and into something beyond that. I told my body to roll fast. It listened and the next kick missed my head. I threw a kick of my own and caught the figure in the general area of the stomach. He let out a pained groan and something clanged near my head. He had a heavy object and was trying to spread what was left of my brains over the 400 section of the St. Bartholomew Library.

Enough is usually enough, though I've found it amazing how much more than enough the human body can take. I scrambled to my knees, ignoring the pain in the injured one, and threw my arms around the guy who was trying to kill me. He took another swing with his piece of metal, but I was too close and he caught me on the fleshy part of my buttocks. In desperation, I sank my teeth into his stomach. He shrieked and shouted, "You crazy bastard!"

"I'm a crazy bastard?" I panted. "Who's trying to kill who?"

I got to my feet and brought my head up hard in the general direction of his chin. I made contact with about the same spot on my cranium he had softened in the parking lot of the New Moon Restaurant. He groaned and I let go of him. We both backed away. I was seeing flashes of color. I didn't think either one of us wanted to go at it again, but something was at stake for both of us. I could see him take a shadowy step toward me, and I got ready to meet him, knowing that I'd never be able to run away and that to turn my back would be my end.

The only thing I could hear was our heavy breathing in the darkness. Then above us a voice.

"What is going on down there, Hill?" shouted the dry librarian from the upper world.

My enemy's head turned upward toward the sound and caught a shaft of light. I saw the face clearly and knew I wouldn't forget it. I also knew I had never seen it before. He turned and ran into the darkness, the faint light of the grillwork making a rippling pattern on his retreating back.

I made my way upward toward the complaining voice of the librarian and met him on the first level.

"What on earth was going on down there?" he demanded.

"Something was going on," I panted, "but I don't think it's reasonable to say it was on earth."

"And where," he demanded further, "is Mr. Hill?"

"I have no idea. He was no part of it. I was attacked by the devil and saved by Saint Bartholomew."

"Dr. Chadwick, have you been drinking?"

"No," I said, leaning against a nearby heavy oak table, "but I did lose a gun down there. I heard it drop down."

"Professors at UCLA carry guns?" he asked, but this time it wasn't a question for me but for himself. "I think I had best call the police."

"What about my gun?"

"It would take some time to search the lower level," he replied, heading back for his desk. "We plan a cleaning tomorrow. If there is a gun there, you can retrieve it."

There was no changing his mind, so gunless I returned to the afternoon. The face of the man who attacked me on level two was about forty, thin, and frenzied. The body that went with it was agile and able. I wouldn't forget either one.

I tried to put the pieces together on the way to Lugosi's house, but they wouldn't fit, not yet. My two cases kept getting in each other's way. When it came to figuring out my expenses, assuming I lived long enough to do that, there would be a lot of items I wasn't sure of. For example, I didn't know whom my friend in St. Bart's library belonged to, though he seemed more out of a Lugosi film than a Faulkner novel.

When I got to Lugosi's house, I found Jeremy Butler on the lawn showing the kid next door how to get a stranglehold.

"The boy spotted me," Butler said. "I told him and his mom I was working for Lugosi, special protection from the Japanese."

"He's a good wrestler," the boy told me, looking at Butler.

"I know," I said.

I asked Jeremy to stick it out for a few more hours and go home if everything looked quiet. He said he would, and I left, wondering how Lugosi would explain the bodyguard to his neighbors. I figured the truth would be best, but since I seldom used it, I didn't see how I could wish it on others.

It was almost six when I got to my office. Shelly was just closing up.

"One message," he said. "I left it on your phone. I'll clean up tomorrow."

For Shelly, there was always tomorrow. The office got cleaned up every three or four months by Jeremy Butler, who couldn't tolerate the mess and potential breeding ground for vermin. Each time Jeremy cleaned the place, Shelly complained and threatened to move out because his "system" had been disrupted.

"That guy with the fang problem," he said, heading for the door and pushing his glasses up on his nose, "is nuts. Good teeth, but they'll be gone in a year, maybe two. I'll probably have to pull them. Man was not meant to wear fangs. If God had wanted man to wear fangs, he would have given us fangs. You wouldn't have to buy them at a costume shop, for God's sake. Is it raining out there?"

"No," I said, shaking the coffee pot on the counter. There

was only a rancid remnant in the pot, but the heat was still on. I turned it off.

"What was I saying?" Shelly asked.

"Fangs," I reminded him.

"Yes, fangs," he said, shaking his head. "If . . . but what's the sense in talking? I'll do what I can. How was your day?"

"All right," I said as he opened the door and looked around as if he had forgotten something. "I almost shot a guy. I was attacked by a lunatic in the library, and I lost my gun."

"Right," said Shelly. "See you tomorrow."

"See you tomorrow, Shel."

He closed the door and I went into my office. The phone message was from Bedelia Sue Frye. She wanted me to call her back. I looked out the window. It was almost dark. I had no intention of talking to her at night.

Then I called Levy's on Spina and asked for Carmen. I had almost sixty dollars of my clients' money left and a nightclub to go to as part of my expenses. I invited Carmen, but she had to work.

"Can I pick you up after work?" I said.

"I'm on till two in the morning," she said. "And after nine hours on my feet, I don't feel like playing games with you. I'm off Wednesday."

"Great," I said. "How about a movie?"

"What happened to the nightclub?" she asked.

"We'll see," I said. "I gotta go now, important client just came in."

I hung up, looked around the office, folded Bedelia Sue Frye's message. I tried the Alexandra Hotel again. This time they told me that Camile Shatzkin's playmate Thayer Newcomb had checked out.

With the sun going down and my .38 gone, I went home carefully, got rid of my empty holster, showered, shaved, and shared a thirty-nine-cent can of Spam with Gunther. I asked

Gunther whether he wanted to go to a nightclub, but he said he had too much work. I almost considered asking Mrs. Plaut.

I caught "A Man Called X" on the radio. Herbert Marshall was telling Leon Belasco where to find some hidden papers. Herbert Marshall always sounded sure of himself. Herbert Marshall had a lot of writers.

Just before nine I made myself as presentable as possible, even changed to my emergency tie, and drove off to Glendale. I knew Glendale. I had grown up there, worked in my old man's grocery store there, been a cop there. It had some pockets of near-poverty along its commercial strip, but Glendale was mainly rising middle class and easy hills. On the borders where it touched other towns, like Burbank, it had a potential blight it couldn't ignore.

The Red Herring was a nightclub on the border. The proprietor called the place a nightclub, but it was really a medium-sized saloon that had gone through a lot of hands and a lot of names. I remembered picking up a kid thief with a broken bottle hiding under the bar there when I was a cop. Two owners ago was a guy named Steele, whom I knew and who disappeared one night and never came back.

The Red Herring was the mailing address of the only member of the Dark Knights of Transylvania I hadn't talked to, Simon Derrida. The place wasn't exactly in a delirium of gaiety when I walked in. There was a barkeeper, two guys at the bar, a couple at one of the six tables, and four guys at another table. The guys wore suits and looked like salesmen. The couple looked like a guy and a pro hustler. Behind them was a small curtained platform and a piano standing empty.

I walked up to the bar and asked for Simon Derrida.

"He's on in about two minutes," the bartender said, consulting his watch. "What'll you have?"

I ordered a Rainier, took it past the fish-eyed drunk at the bar, who eyed me like he wanted to talk, and went to one of the empty tables.

The woman at the next table looked over at me to see whether I was a better possibility than the guy she had and I shook my head no. She had lots of red hair that wouldn't stay in place and a smile painted on her large mouth that promised more sadness than fun.

I was almost through with my beer when a guy with a ratty tux came out from behind the curtain and sat at the piano. He was about seventy. He smiled at the four businessmen, the woman, and me and began playing and singing.

He played "Jealous," doing a kind of Tony Martin imitation, and followed it with "Chattanooga Choo-Choo" and a finger flourish. I clapped. The businessmen clapped, and the guy at the piano beamed.

"Thank you very much, ladies and gentlemen. Now let's all sing 'We'll Throw the Japs Back in the Laps of the Nazis.' "

He began to play and sing, but no one joined him. Undiscouraged, he tried to feed us the lines quickly before he played them. I mouthed a little, and the drunk at the bar followed us both by four muddled lines. If the old duck at the piano played another song, I was going to go to the bathroom, but he didn't. Instead, he thanked us all again and said, "And now, the man you've all been waiting for, the man who can scare you and tickle you to death at the same time, our own Doctor Vampire, Simon Derrida."

He played "Hall of the Mountain King" to applause from the drunk, and the last Dark Knight walked out on the platform, complete with the costume he had worn at the meeting. He couldn't cover his New York accent, though he tried and came up with an awful combination of Bela Lugosi and the Bronx.

"Good evening," he said. "It's good to see some fresh blood in the club. I'm going to give you some stories in a new vein. My friends, do you know what is worse than a werewolf who had to get rabies shots? A vampire who has to get braces."

The drunk burped.

"And," Derrida went on with a flourishing of his cape (he looked more like a dry pear than a vampire), "do you know why the vampire walked around in his pajamas? He didn't have a batrobe. Quick, what has one wheel and gets twenty miles to the gallon of plasma? A vampire on a unicycle. Or tell me what the first building is that Dracula visits when he goes to New York? The Vampire State Building."

No one was laughing. Nobody but the drunk and me were really listening. I had a fixed smile, and Derrida started to play to me, which forced me to pay attention and fake a laugh. He didn't seem to recognize me from the Dark Knights meeting. My hope was that his act was short or that he would be discouraged by the lack of response, but he just plowed on even when he asked, "What do vampires hate to have for dinner?" and the drunk answered, "T-bone stakes." Derrida simply ignored him and delivered the line again.

"Why don't you like Count Dracula?" Derrida asked an imaginary character at his side. Then he moved over, raised his voice and answered, "Because he's a pain in the neck."

I squirmed through, "Why did the man think Dracula had a cold? Because the vampire told him he kept a coffin," and "What do you get if you cross a vampire with a brontosaurus? A monster that sleeps in the biggest coffin you ever saw." Then I had a simulated coughing fit that sent me to the men's room, which was small, dirty, and without toilet paper, but at least I didn't have to bear the pain of being Simon Derrida's sole emotional support. The burden was too much.

I stayed in the toilet till I heard about three people clapping, which could mean only that Derrida was done. I hurried out and ducked behind the curtain. "Just a second," he said and stepped out for more applause. The drunk and the hustler applauded and Derrida came "backstage," which was just big enough to hold us.

"Great show," I said. "Can I buy you a drink?"

Derrida smiled, "It did go pretty well, didn't it? Not a bad audience for a weekday."

We went back to my table, completely ignored, while the old guy at the piano played "Always."

"I'll have a double scotch," Derrida shouted to the bartender.

"Another beer for me," I added.

"I know you from somewhere," Derrida said, looking at me.

"Dark Knights," I said. "I was there with Lugosi."

"Inspiring man," Derrida said solemnly. "Gave me lots of ideas for new material just looking at him. I'm getting my imitation down perfect. What do you think?"

"Uncanny," I said.

"So," he said, sitting back and throwing his cape over the chair, "you found me out. It was bound to happen. Hell, you expect that kind of thing in show business. Heartaches, disaster. You gotta learn to live with it. I got enough material out of them, anyway."

"You mean," I said as the bartender plopped the drinks on the table and stood waiting for his pay, "that you don't believe in the Dark Knights?"

"Use 'em for material, that's all. Too bad you happened to come in tonight. I could have gotten a little more out of them."

That made everyone in the Dark Knights except Sam Billings a fraud. A fang overbite and no true friends.

"I didn't just happen in here," I said. "I was looking for you."

I told him my tale.

"You think I was putting the bite on Lugosi?" he said. "Get that joke?"

"I got it," I said, gulping my beer. "I considered it, but I think you're off my list."

"Why?" he said. "Say, I can be scary too, not just funny if I want to be, buddy."

"I can see that," I said, "but you're a trooper. A professional. You wouldn't stiff another professional."

That worked.

"Right," he said seriously, finishing his drink. "Say, I wish I could help you but I've got nothing going. Why don't you stay around for the second show? I have new material for part of it."

"I don't think so," I said. "I've got a big day tomorrow. By the way, I don't plan to turn you in to Billings. I think he needs you more than you need him."

"I don't get you, pal," Derrida said.

"Skip it," I said and headed for the door.

The drunk waved. The bartender read a book. The red-head talked, and the old guy at the piano tinkled. I walked out the door and headed for my car.

The sound of screeching rubber came from the parking lot of the rival tavern across the street. I paid no attention and kept on walking till I realized that the car had crossed the street and was coming down the sidewalk right behind me. I faked a move to the wall and took a dive toward the street, feeling the pull in my knee. The car swerved and passed me, and a bullet chunked a piece of street near my face. There were two figures in the Ford. I couldn't see the driver, but the guy in the passenger seat was my attacker from the library.

I waited to see whether they were going to make another try, and sure enough I heard the car turning down the street and saw its lights. Fear was gone. I was hit with anger. Someone was trying to kill me, and they were going to keep at it till it worked unless I did something about it. Now seemed a good time to do something. I rolled into the shadow next to the car I had dived over and wormed my way to my Buick while the Ford eased forward, looking for me. I crawled to the sidewalk side, opened the door as little as I could, slid in, and started the engine as soon as the Ford pulled past. I got into the street with a tear of rubber and put on my bright lights. I could see the two figures ahead of me and they realized now I was behind them. It was a time for madness, and I sped forward, ramming into the rear of the Ford, sending it jerking ahead and snapping the heads of the two guys in the front seat.

The hell with my Buick. It was a discardable weapon now, and I meant to use it. The driver of the Ford decided to wait for a better day and stepped on the gas, but I had no intention of giving him a better day. The night was mine and I meant to have it.

I chased them through Burbank and into the hills. Not a cop showed up to stop us, and that was fine with me. We went through Griffith Park and far beyond. We ran red lights and missed pedestrians. The only thing that was going to stop me was a bullet or an empty gas tank.

Then I lost them. I cursed the car, my brother, my stupidity, and fate. I didn't even know where we were. I knew it was a poorly lighted street with small apartments. I drove slowly down the street, watching and listening. Nothing. Then I heard a car backfire or a shot and went around the block, where I spotted the Ford under a street lamp. Its doors were open. No one was in sight.

I drove next to the car and got out. Instead of going to the Ford, I went to the trunk and got out my tire iron. The Ford was empty, but in the light from the lamp I could see blood, a lot of blood on the seat, particularly the passenger side. There was a dark trail leading from the Ford. I began to follow it, tire iron in hand. The moon was full above, and I began to regain my sense of self-preservation and fear, but I followed the trail of blood to an apartment house door. Then it hit me. I thought I was having one of those feelings where you think you've been someplace you've never been, but I'd been here. I'd been here in the daytime and talked to a janitor named Rouse.

I went in and rang Rouse's bell. He came into the hall with his shirt and mouth open and unlatched the hall door.

"I just called you two minutes ago," he said. "How did you . . . ?"

"Upstairs?" I said.

"Yeah, someone's up there."

Then he noticed the trail of blood leading up the stairs into the darkness and the tire iron in my hand.

"I'll give you the five when I come down," I said, moving to the stairs slowly.

"Mister," said Rouse, "you keep your five. I'm calling the cops."

He disappeared into his apartment, locking the door behind him. The blood trail led right to the door of the apartment Camile Shatzkin had rented as Mrs. Offen. The door was open and the lights were out. I moved in slowly, kicking the door closed, and standing back with tire iron ready in case anyone was behind it. No one was. There was enough light from the street to follow the blood, but I reached over and turned on the wall light, tire iron ready.

The trail led toward the single bedroom. I followed it, kicking that door open. He was there. The guy who had jumped me in the library and tried to kill me in the Ford. He was on the bed staring at me, but he wasn't seeing anything. A wooden stake was imbedded in his chest, and his dead hands were clutching it in a final useless effort to wrench it out.

CHAPTER EIGHT

Before the police arrived, I went through the unpleasant pockets of the guy on the bed and found that he was Thayer Newcomb. That was two down for Mrs. Shatzkin and a little confusing for me. The apartment and Newcomb were tied to the Shatzkin murder, but Newcomb had acted more like a Dark Knight of Transylvania than a plotting lover. The stake in his chest seemed to confirm the vampire line, and the neatly typed card in his wallet, albeit a bit blood-stained, didn't help at all. The card bore the exact words of the threat Lugosi had received over the phone. I returned the wallet, complete with fifteen bucks, put my tire iron on a lower shelf in the kitchen, and waited for the screaming siren.

It came in about fifteen minutes. Heavy footsteps thundered up the stairs, a heavier knock hit the door.

"Police," said a high voice.

"Come in," said I, sitting on the sofa with both hands showing.

They came in with guns out, blue caps over their eyes, ready to create more blood trails if someone said the wrong thing. I said the right thing.

"In the bedroom," I said.

One guy was young, in his twenties, and looked as if he had tailored his uniform at his own expense to the body he had probably built up as a high school athlete. When I was young and twenty, I thought, looking at his frightened blue eyes. Cop Number Two was older by ten years, heavier by twenty pounds, and possessed of a skin that looked as if it had suffered a blast of BB shot when he was a kid. The older cop went into the bedroom. The younger one prepared to kill me if I scratched my nose.

"There's a dead guy in there," the cop with the bad skin said, coming out.

"I know," I said.

"I was telling my partner," he said.

"Sorry."

The partner kid ran into the bedroom, holding his holster in his free hand to keep it from slapping his thigh. He came out fast.

"He's dead," he said. "What do we do?"

"Call the cops," I suggested.

"You're not funny, guy," said the older cop. "Where's the phone?"

"None in here," I told him. "Downstairs, janitor has one."

The younger guy hurried downstairs, and the older guy kept his hand on his gun.

"What happened?" he said.

"Beats the hell out of me," I said.

A little over an hour later, after I watched the guys from the evidence lab try to figure out the difference between what was evidence and what was junk dropped by the cops, I was on my way to the Wilshire District station. I had told the cop who questioned me that the murder was tied into a case being conducted by an Officer Cawelti. The cop called Cawelti and was glad to dump the case in his lap along with me and his report. He had his own big problem, a tire theft gang, and as far as he was concerned, with the shortage of rubber, that was more important than actors getting murdered.

"Actors have been getting murdered and killing themselves in this town for half a century," the cop told me philosophically while he chewed a wad of gum.

I told him that was true, though I didn't see what that had to do with his disinterest.

At the Wilshire station Cawelti, his hair still parted down the middle and slicked down, stood up when I was ushered into the squad room. There were a few cops in the room, and I thought I heard the sound of voices from my brother's office. A big cardboard box that had held sandwiches rested on one nearby desk. From the smell I could tell they had come from a delicatessen.

Cawelti took the report from the officer, who said, "You're welcome."

"What do you want?" said Cawelti, "A tip?"

"I'll give you one," said the cop who had brought me in. "Some day you might run into me again when you need a favor. Think about that."

"Guys," I said sweetly. "There's been a murder."

The cop who had brought me turned in disgust and walked out. Cawelti threw me a snarl. I smiled at him as sweetly as I could, and he turned to read the report. It took him about three minutes. He didn't read it twice. He should have.

"Why did you kill him?" he said, looking up at me.

"He was dead when I got there," I said. "I met the building janitor downstairs, and we saw a trail of blood. I followed it. The janitor's information is in the report."

"You probably stabbed him with that wood spear and followed him up there to be sure he was dead," he tried.

"Then I waited for the cops to come," I said.

"Why not?" he said, leaning back with his hands behind his head. He wanted me to squirm, but I wasn't playing it.

"Come on," I said, "I was on a case. I think this guy had something to do with the Shatzkin murder."

"The guy Faulkner shot," he said.

"Mrs. Shatzkin rented the apartment where the body was

found, and according to her, the dead guy was her boyfriend. Take out both your hands and all your pinkies and add it up. It comes out to a pile of rotten fish."

"It comes out to your pipe dreams," said Cawelti, leaning forward to tap at the report.

"Why not ask Mrs. Shatzkin about her boyfriend and check with the janitor? Show him her picture."

"She jabbed the spear into this guy Newcomb?"

"I don't think so," I said. "It might have been a monster who laps at her heels named Haliburton. He was jealous. Maybe he found out about Newcomb earlier today."

"Mrs. Shatzkin sure plays around a lot," Cawelti said with acrid sarcasm. "Even if you're right, what about Shatzkin's dying statement that Faulkner killed him?"

"I'm working on that," I said, looking over at my brother's door, which had just opened. He and Seidman walked out. Cawelti spotted them and sat forward businesslike, finding a pencil.

"And what were you doing following that Thayer guy into the Culver City apartment?" Cawelti said evenly, letting his eyes but not his head turn toward the advancing Phil and Seidman.

"I promised the janitor a five if he called me when he heard anyone go in the apartment."

Phil and Seidman were in easy earshot now.

Cawelti attacked.

"Rouse called you, left a message at your boarding house, and you arrived two minutes later? And you live over on Heliotrope in Hollywood? You made good time."

"I was trailing Newcomb. He had tried to run me down because I was getting too close to him. I was protecting some innocent cop like you who should have been digging up what I was digging up and worrying Newcomb instead of sitting here trying to prove what it means to be a true pisshead."

Cawelti started to get up and threw a look at Phil, who

didn't move, just watched without a word. Seidman looked at his watch.

"You got a report on whatever's going on here?" Phil asked as Cawelti reached forward and grabbed my jacket, pulling me out of the wooden chair. The chair went skidding across the squad room, ramming the table with deli refuse and sending it tumbling along the floor, where it would feel right at home.

Cawelti paused but didn't take his eyes from mine or his fist from my jacket.

"Let him go," Seidman said softly.

Cawelti looked at Phil, who had moved to his desk to get the report.

"Do what you think best," Phil said, looking down at the report and loosening his tie to the point that it was no longer tied at all.

What Cawelti thought was best was to throw an open fist at my face. It caught my nose and cheek and a corner of my eye. I spun around and started to fall but grabbed the edge of the desk. I knew I had wanted Cawelti to do that and that I was going to hit him as hard and fast as I could, but I was too late. Phil had moved around Cawelti's desk like a handball on a hard court and had him by the neck.

Cawelti's bewildered face turned red and then redder as he tried to pry Phil's fingers off.

"You ever touch him again," he said through teeth that looked as if they would break from the pressure, "you won't be able to eat anything but jello for a long time. You understand?"

Cawelti tried to talk, but Phil's hands around his neck wouldn't let him. He was turning slowly from red to blue.

"Phil," Seidman said without moving, "Enough."

Somewhere deep inside, Phil heard and slowly responded, letting Cawelti slip from his reluctant thick fingers. The part in his hair showed Cawelti's crimson scalp as he staggered back against a desk.

I didn't say anything.

"Come with us," Phil said over his shoulder in my general direction and went to the door with Seidman trailing back to be sure I didn't throw one at Cawelti, who was choking.

"I think you have a sore throat," Seidman said to Cawelti. "Go on home, gargle, stay in bed till noon tomorrow."

Hate would have been bliss compared to the look Cawelti shot me as he staggered back to his desk, gasping and holding his neck. I limped quickly and caught up with Seidman and Phil, who was reading the Newcomb report as we walked.

"Phil," I said.

"Shut up," he hissed, going down the stairs. "Just shut up. I don't like what I just did, and I may do it to you, which I would like. So shut up."

"We're on a call," Seidman said as we went through the lobby, stepping over an overturned garbage can that almost blocked the doorway.

"Clean this thing up, Swartz," Phil shouted at the old cop on the desk.

"I'm Clayton," the old guy shot back, "and it didn't happen on my shift. Some guy tried to run. Swartz should have cleaned it. If I stopped and . . ."

Phil stopped and turned to face Clayton, who shut up.

"I'll clean it up now, Lieutenant," he said softly, and out we went into a car at the curb.

When we were in the car with Seidman driving and Phil next to me in the back seat, Phil put down the report and said, "Now talk. No jokes, no lies, no errors and you'll have a no-hitter."

I talked as we shot through the early morning darkness, headed I didn't know where. I told him the truth from start to finish including the Shatzkin and Lugosi material.

"So," said Phil, "what do you make of it?"

"I don't know," I said. "There's no link between the two cases. It's crazy."

"There's a link," said Seidman from the front seat. I could see his sunken-eyed skull of a face in the rearview mirror.

"Yeah," I said. "Me. I'm the missing link."

"And . . . ?" said Phil.

"I'll work on it," I said.

"How's your knee?" Phil said, turning his head away from me out the window.

That was the blow I almost couldn't handle. My mind went blank, and I reviewed more than four decades of life with Phil. Three had never been anything like this.

"Ruth told me," he explained.

"Told you?"

"The money," he said.

Seidman pretended to hear nothing.

"I thought you'd break my head if you found out," I said.

Phil's hands were in his lap. They wanted to do something, but his mind was stopping him.

"I don't like it," he said, "but I need it."

"Then why are you holding your hands like that? If I forgot your words, I'd think you wanted to crush my head."

"Different reason," he said. "You scared the hell out of Dave. You were supposed to take him to see *Dumbo*. You took him to see some zombie movie. He had nightmares last night. You forget he almost died last year after the car hit him? He's eight years old and living with the idea that he was almost killed."

"I was wrong," I said quietly.

"You've been wrong ninety-nine times out of one hundred since you were . . ."

"Since I was eight," I finished. "Where are we going?"

"Mrs. Shatzkin's friend Haliburton just had an accident," said Seidman.

We didn't say anything more. Seidman drove and turned on the police radio to break the pained silence. It purred numbers and addresses to us, soothed us with reports of vandalism and possible mayhem, made us think about something besides ourselves.

We got where we were going in about ten minutes. It was a downtown hotel on Main Street a few doors from the bus depot. A sign outside said rooms were two dollars and up, with separate bath.

When we hit the lobby, the desk clerk came around the counter and moved toward us, his mouth open to speak. Phil held up his hand to stop him from saying anything and told Seidman, "Talk to him."

A young cop, his face pale, sweat on his collar and his LAPD badge new and shiny, was waiting at the elevator. The lobby, which wasn't much beyond some sagging stuffed chairs and three stunted palms, was empty.

"Elevator's out, Lieutenant," the young cop said. "I'm Officer Rnzini. The crime was on the fourth floor."

"I think I can walk it without a heart attack," Phil shot back.

"I didn't mean . . ." Rnzini began, but Phil was already taking the stairs two at a time, trying not to pant. I followed behind Rnzini, trying not to smell the building's rancidness.

"It's crazy," Rnzini whispered confidentially to me but loud enough for Phil to hear. "The guy looks like he was shotgunned, but he was alone in a locked room, window locked tight, looks like it hasn't been opened in years. Doesn't make any sense."

Phil stopped suddenly on the stairs, and Rnzini had to throw himself against the wall to keep from bumping into my brother, who looked like an angry refrigerator. Phil had stopped to catch his breath, but he masked the reason by turning on the cop behind him.

"Maybe you did it," he said. "Just to confuse the police department. Maybe you're bored. Maybe seeing crime has warped your brain."

Rnzini started to smile and stopped. Phil wasn't smiling.

"Lieutenant, I'm Catholic," he said seriously.

"Of course," Phil answered and started up the stairs again. Rnzini stayed a bit farther behind him.

There was a small crowd on the fourth floor and a sleepy uniformed cop standing outside a room with a door snapped off its hinges. The cop woke up.

"You talk to all these people?" Phil said over his shoulder.

"All the ones who admit hearing anything," Rnzini said, catching up.

Phil elbowed his way past two young Mexican kids. One of them turned an angry face, and Phil looked back at him.

"Something on your mind, Chico?" he said.

The two kids backed away.

Inside the small room, Phil looked around, but there was no doubt what we were drawn to. The body on the bed.

"That Haliburton?" he said to me.

I walked over to the body. Shotgun victims do not look peaceful, and depending on how close the shotgun was, they may not look like anything at all. Haliburton still had his face. He was also clutching a .45 in his right hand.

"That's him," I said.

"Your notebook," Phil spat at Rnzini and pulled it out of the hands of the sweating young cop before he could hand it over. Phil moved into the small washroom and read it through slowly. Rnzini stood next to me, trying not to breathe or think. In a few minutes, Sergeant Seidman came into the room and looked around. There was no change in his expression when he looked at Haliburton's big body on the bed.

I had told Haliburton to pack and leave earlier, and it looked as if he might have taken my advice, but he hadn't run fast enough or far enough. Seidman walked into the washroom, and Phil got off the toilet seat, handing him the notebook. I followed Seidman and watched Phil take off his tie, stuff it in his pocket and sit on the bed next to the dead man but far enough away to keep from getting bloody.

"He had that gun in his hand and the door locked because he was afraid that someone might be looking for him who wished him no good," said Phil. "Make sense to you, Rnzini?"

I read the notes over Seidman's shoulder. It was printed carefully in neat letters and easy to read. After the preliminary business about time and call, it consisted mainly of a statement from a witness, a Richard A. Mann, 1488 Sagamore Drive, Cleveland, Ohio.

The statement read:

"My name is Richard A. Mann. I live at 1488 Sagamore Drive in Cleveland, Ohio. I'm a salesman, costume jewelry. I usually stay at the cheapest clean hotel I can find. You know, profit margin, but I've been a little down in sales. I'm not the only one. No one's sure what's going to happen with the war. They don't want to buy. Tell the truth, if I knew just how bad this place really was, I wouldn't have stayed.

"It was just about one in the morning, maybe an hour ago. Couldn't sleep. Read the news and Li'l Abner. Got up, lathered my face for a shave. Threw a towel around my neck. This place is made out of balsa wood. The guy above me had been pacing back and forth. I had half a mind to go up and tell him to sit down, but I've had nights like that on the road, you know. So, I figured, let the guy alone. Maybe he's got enough troubles. Live and let live.

"I was in the room by the bed, shaving cream on my face, you know. Not much room to wander with one small room and that little bathroom. I could tell exactly where the guy upstairs was, and I'm sure the guy below me knows where I was. Well, I was standing next to the bed deciding whether to watch the wallpaper peel for a few hours or listen to the radio after I shaved when I heard the shots. Loud, real loud. And I knew right away where they came from. A blast and an echo. For a second, I thought the building's boiler blew. Probably happen some day. Radiator's rattling all night. It probably hasn't been checked in years. Well, there I was, ready to shave, just standing there for a second. I put everything down and went out into the hall. My face was still covered with cream, towel over my shoulder, you know.

"The Belvedere doesn't have a lot of curious tenants. In a place like this, and I've been in plenty of them, people have their own problems and aren't about to get into anyone else's troubles. But there were a few people in the hall. One old guy with white whiskers looked like a scared bird. He had on an undershirt with a big hole in it. His mouth was open like he was trying to say something, but nothing came out.

" 'Shots upstairs,' I said, and went for the stairs. Maybe I should have minded my own business, but I didn't think. The pacing guy might have killed himself or someone else. Those shots were too damn close.

"The stairs sagged as I went up. You can see I'm not a little guy, but hotel stairs should be made to hold a lot more than me. This whole damn place is coming apart. When I got up to the fourth floor there were maybe three, four people in the hall. One woman looked like . . . well, officer, you know this place better than I do. Most of the doors were closed and quiet, like they hadn't heard what they must have heard.

" 'In there,' I told them, and I pointed at the door of the room above mine. I must have looked like a foaming screwball. They backed away, and I knocked on the door. No answer. The door was locked. I told everyone in the hall to get back and I went with my shoulder against the door. It snapped away, banging open. I think my ten-year-old daughter could have gone through it. Then I saw him. Lying on the bed covered the way he is now. I'll never forget it. I went back into the hall before any of the others could see it. I was sorry I had seen it. I told the nearest guy, a thin guy in his sixties I think, to call a cop. Then I went back into the room to see if he might still be alive. Believe me, I didn't want to check and I didn't think he could be, but you know, there might have been a chance. He was dead. I yelled at the people in the hall not to come in, not to touch anything, and I just waited till you got here. Now if there's nothing else, officer, I'm feeling kind of shaky, and I'd like to get back to my room and clean up. If you need me, I'll be in the room right below."

It was the most unnecessarily complete statement I had ever seen. It must have been Rnzini's first murder, and he didn't want to leave anything out. If he stayed a cop, the reports would get sloppier and sloppier and reach a point where they'd start getting better again or deteriorate to where he'd be one of the crowd.

"You know who killed this guy, Rnzini?" Phil said, looking straight at the young cop.

"No," Rnzini answered. He looked like he was going to giggle and confess himself.

"You should," sighed Phil. "By God, you should."

"He's right," said Seidman, coming back into the room and handing the notebook back to Rnzini.

"It's right in your book, kid," I said.

Rnzini looked at his notebook, wondering whether someone had written something inside it he hadn't seen.

Without looking at the body, Phil said in a rumble of familiar anger, "Look at our friend Haliburton on the bed here. Pellet holes in him with a narrow pattern, powerful. Pellet holes in his feet, from the bottom up. Strike you as strange, Rnzini?"

"He was shot while he was lying on the bed?" Rnzini tried.

"No pellet holes in the bed by his feet. Lots of blood, but no holes. Blood on the floor," said Seidman, looking around the room and at the floor.

"Someone moved him, Rnzini," said Phil, looking at the wall. "Any idea who?"

"It wasn't me," Rnzini said defensively.

"Well, that eases my mind and narrows the list of suspects," Phil said. "Any ideas beyond that?"

"You've got a guy alone in a room," Seidman picked up the conversation. "He's got a gun and he's afraid someone is after him. Suppose you were after him and found him here. What would you do?"

Rnzini tried to think, but nothing came, nothing except a look that showed that being a cop might not be such a good profession after all.

"Rnzini," Phil interrupted.

"I don't know, Lieutenant."

"Well, in a tin-can hotel like this," Phil said, looking at the circular imitation Oriental rug on the floor that had long since lost its pattern, "you might get a room next door or below or above the guy you were after. You might get a shotgun with a hell of a kick, listen to our old friend Haliburton here pace the floor for a few minutes, figure out where he was standing and send a blast through the wall or floor or ceiling. You wouldn't have to be too accurate. You see any holes in the walls or ceiling, Rnzini?"

Rnzini looked. There was nothing.

"Five will get you ten if you move that dime-store Chinese rug, you'll find some holes in the floor," said Phil.

"Mr. Mann from downstairs?" said Rnzini.

Phil winked sourly, and Rnzini got on his knees and moved the rug. The pattern of holes in the floor under it was almost symmetrical. The room below was dark.

"Mr. Mann," I began, "put shaving cream on his face, threw a towel over his shoulder, stood on a chair, and put the blast on Haliburton, who must have been surprised as hell."

"He put down the shotgun," Seidman continued, "ran out in the hall, and started to yell about the gunshot upstairs before anyone had a chance to think or say that the shot might have come from his room. He went up the stairs and got to the door of Haliburton's room, broke it down and told everyone to get away and call the cops. He wanted to make sure Haliburton was dead and to buy himself some time. He put the body on the bed, moved the rug to cover the holes, and waited for you to show up. Then he told you his story."

"But," said Rnzini, "why the shaving cream?"

"Hide his face," I said. "He could wear a mask right in front of you. He probably used his towel to move the body, keep from getting blood on him. Then he just walked into the washroom over there and took another clean towel. Bloody one's probably under the body or the bed. Then he gave you his story, walked down to his room, grabbed his already packed bag, if he even had one, and went out the door."

One of the two forty-watt bulbs in the ceiling fixture sputtered and died. Phil pointed downward.

"We can go downstairs now and find an empty room and no fingerprints," he said. "Then we can start doing legwork."

"I didn't . . ." Rnzini started.

"You didn't ask enough questions," Phil said wearily. "You weren't suspicious enough. You didn't make everyone sit down someplace where you could keep an eye on them. You get a crime and witnesses, you sit them down where you can see them till someone who knows what he's doing shows up. I don't care if it's your mother or your priest."

Rnzini had nothing to say. Phil got off the bed slowly and walked out of the room into the hall. I stayed long enough to give Rnzini a look of sympathy.

"My brother and old man have a dry cleaning business in Pasadena," he said. "I could go in with them."

"Your report was good, really good," I said.

"What's with him, anyway?" Rnzini said, nodding in the general direction of my departed brother.

"He's a cop," I said. "If you stick around a couple of dozen years, you've got a chance at being as good a cop and as miserable a man as he is. It comes with the badge."

By the time I caught up with Phil and Seidman, they were already back in the lobby, leaning on the desk clerk, who looked surprisingly unseedy for the Belvedere. His suit was wrinkled but a suit nonetheless. It looked better than mine. His tie was neat. His dead giveaway was the stubble on his face. He needed a touch of grime and that was it. His face was pale and somewhere between twenty-five and forever years old, with a few strands of dark hair combed, brushed, and plastered forward to give himself and no one else the illusion that something was growing up there.

"Haliburton checked in at one in the morning?" Seidman said, consulting his notebook. It was almost dawn.

"Yes," said the clerk.

"And Mr. Mann in 303?" Seidman continued. Phil simply stood with his arms crossed, looking angry. The clerk couldn't keep his eyes from him.

"Let's see," he said, finding a pair of glasses and checking his register. "Checked in a few minutes later. Said he was a colleague of Mr. Haliburton and wanted a room very near him. I gave him 303 right below, which didn't seem . . ."

"What did he look like?" Seidman interrupted.

"Mr. Haliburton?" asked the clerk.

"Mann."

"Glasses, dark mustache, hat tilted forward, a fairly large man, not as large as Mr. Haliburton," said the clerk.

"Think you could identify Mann again without the hat, glasses, and mustache?" asked Seidman.

"Without . . . I don't know. I didn't really stare at him. We were busy at the time . . ."

"Thanks," said Seidman, closing his notebook.

"Our killer has flair," I said as we walked back to the car. "A wooden spear in the stomach and a shotgun blast through a floor."

"If the same guy did both these jobs tonight," Phil said.

"It's possible," I said, getting into the car.

"You thought Billy Conn was going to beat Joe Louis," Phil reminded me. "I think we should talk to Mrs. Shatzkin."

Seidman nodded. The sun was definitely coming up and it was Tuesday. On the way to Bel Air we stopped at a stand for coffee and some sinkers. The guy had no cereal. I looked at the counterman's newspaper while he read it and caught only the headline that said the United States had sunk a Japanese warship and crippled a battleship from a secret air base near Manila.

It was just before seven when we got to the front door of the Shatzkin house. Phil knocked instead of pressing the bell. The Mexican maid answered. She was wearing a robe and a yawn.

"Mrs. Shatzkin is still sleeping," she whispered.

"Wake her up," Phil said.

"But . . ."

"But hell," Phil shouted, *"Tiene prisa.* Move."

The frightened girl moved. We could hear her going up the stairs as we entered the hall. Phil led the way and found the living room. He looked at the furnishings with distaste, probably comparing the place to his own in North Hollywood and not enjoying the comparison and the lack of sleep.

Camile Shatzkin came down in about five minutes. She had taken the time to put on her face and a robin's-egg blue robe that cut a nice *V* at the neckline, which could distract us.

"What is this?" she said.

"We're the scorekeepers," I said.

Phil told me to shut up.

"Mr. Peters says you admitted yesterday to being a close friend of Thayer Newcomb," Phil said. "Is that right?"

"Why yes," she said with a slight fluster and hand movement. "I've known Thayer for . . ."

"And you rented an apartment in Culver City where you could meet him secretly," Phil went on.

Mrs. Shatzkin bit her lower lip prettily.

"I don't see what this has to do with my husband's murder," she said. "If you are going to persist along these lines, I'm going to have to insist that I can say no more until I talk to my lawyer."

"Newcomb is dead," I said.

Phil shot me a look that should have sent me skidding on my heels through the wall.

"Thayer is dead?" she said, putting her right hand up to her throat. "That's awful. How?"

"Someone shoved a wooden stake into his chest," I said.

Phil stepped toward me with a ready fist. I tried to watch him and Camile Shatzkin. I interpreted her look as shock and fear, but I didn't see any grief coming for a lost lover. She sobbed and sat with shaky knees on the nearest chair.

"When did you see Mr. Newcomb last, Mrs. Shatzkin?" Seidman asked, to draw Phil's attention from me.

"I don't know," she said weakly, "Maybe a week, two weeks. I don't know. We were . . . we had decided not to see each other again. I regretted the whole thing. And then Jacques died."

I still didn't see any grief and neither did Phil or Seidman.

"Do you know where Mr. Haliburton is?" Seidman went on.

She looked up in something resembling surprise.

"Why? I mean, he left last night. Quit. He was very devoted to Jacques, almost a son to us. He just couldn't stand being around here. I understood."

If there was any devotion in Haliburton, it had been directed at Mrs. Shatzkin, and if there was maternal love in his looks, Oedipus could move over to make room for one more on the couch.

"Haliburton is dead," I said, taking two steps back from Phil.

Seidman stepped between us and said softly, "Phil, Phil . . . not here."

"He's dead?" Mrs. Shatzkin said with eyes opening in bewilderment.

"Yeah," I said. "Isn't it curious how men who get too close to you wind up dead? The count is three, and the way I see it, there's one left. Care to come up with a name, Camile?"

Camile coughed like her namesake and almost had a fit.

"Maria," she called through the cough, "Maria."

The maid came running in.

"Call Doctor Gartley now. Tell him to come quickly. I'm going to my room."

Without a goodbye or final comment, she made her exit.

"I'd give her one and a half stars on that performance," I said. "She wasn't upset about Newcomb's death, and maybe she knew about Haliburton getting it."

I was waiting for Phil's fist and backed away when I saw it coming out of the corner of my eye. He missed by inches, and I went behind the couch.

"You bastard," he said. "I told you to keep your mouth shut. I wanted to move this thing slowly."

"I've got a client in jail," I said. Seidman was touching Phil's arm to suggest restraint. He wasn't actually going to step in my brother's way if he lost control.

"She's in this with somebody," I said.

"In what?" said Phil. "Shatzkin's murder? Newcomb, Haliburton? Is she keeping busy on the side by threatening Bela Lugosi? It sounds like a cheap movie."

"It does, doesn't it?" I said, getting a germ of an idea. I knew the germ would sprout, grow, and itch until I made something of it.

I sat as far away from Phil in the back seat as I could when we drove back, and I didn't say anything. They parked at the Wilshire station and got out.

"You want me to come upstairs?" I said.

"I think we want you to go away, Toby," Seidman said.

"My car is in Culver City," I said.

"Take a streetcar," Phil said.

"What about Lugosi?" I called at the two detectives going up the stairs.

"We'll put a man on him," Seidman said and disappeared

through the dirty glass doors that caught the sun and sent it dancing in my mind.

I caught the streetcar, paid my nickel, and fell asleep. At the end of the line, the motorman woke me up and I rode back again trying to stay awake. I could easily have become the Flying Dutchman of the Los Angeles transit system. It took me almost an hour to get back to my car.

Since I was there, I dropped in to see Rouse, the janitor.

When he saw me in the hall, he said, "No," and closed his door.

"I left my tire iron upstairs," I shouted.

No answer.

"I owe you five bucks," I shouted. The door opened.

"Give it to me and go," he said, chewing away as he had before. I wondered whether it was food consumption or a nervous habit.

"One last question," I said. "For another five."

Rouse looked toward the stairs.

"I been up hours cleaning that blood," he said. "Didn't get back to sleep. My wife wants to move. Where am I going to get another job?"

"Sorry to hear that," I said. "Did you get a look at the body before they took it out?"

"Yeah," he said, looking up the stairs.

"You recognize him?"

Rouse shrugged.

"I told the police maybe, but there was another guy who went there. Bigger guy, not big-big, but good-sized. I could tell by hearing them over my head. Never got a look at him. I thought he was Mr. Offen."

I gave him the five and said thanks.

"Police said not to touch anything up there," he said. "I'll get your tire iron when I can."

He went back inside. I'd dropped my gun in a library and

my tire iron in an apartment. I checked to be sure my wallet was still in my back pocket. It was.

I drove back home slowly to keep from killing any more Los Angelians and got there by nine. I pulled myself up the stairs, fished out some change, and made some calls. First I called Shelly and told him if he saw Jeremy Butler to tell him to drop the watch on Lugosi. Shelly said I had two more messages from Bedelia Sue Frye. Then I called Lugosi's house and left a message to tell Butler to go home if he showed up. My next call was to my brother. I got Seidman instead.

"Phil's gone home for a few hours," he said. "And I was on the way out. What's up?"

"How about a suggestion for the medical examiner who does the autopsy on Newcomb?" I said. "Have him look for a bullet."

"There was no bullet hole in the corpse," Seidman said. "Just the wooden spike."

"What if there was a bullet hole," I said, holding back a yawn, "but someone didn't want you to know it and . . ."

". . . he shoved the stake in to cover the wound," Seidman completed. "What the hell for?"

"To make it look like a vampire caper," I explained. "To link Newcomb to the Lugosi case. Newcomb had been cropping up and giving me scares. He was working with someone to keep me as far away from the Shatzkin murder and as close to the Lugosi case as possible. Remember, I'm probably the thing that links the two."

"I'll tell the medical examiner," said Seidman. "Anything else?"

There was nothing else. I hung up, drooped to my room, and closed my shades. I put my clothes on the chair near the table and hit the mattress with a roll. I was out before a vampire bat could blink a blind eye.

I dreamed of blood and roses, shaving cream and dark basements. Out of the crash of images, I found myself a little

kid again in the basement below the store my old man had
owned in Glendale. I hated to go down there and get boxes. It
was dark with wooden shelves and places for nightmares to
hide. An old Negro named Maury had slept down there from
time to time. Maury used to help in our store and others in the
neighborhood. Maury died when I was about seven, and I
didn't want to meet his ghost in the basement. In my dream, I
went down and looked around. I wasn't alone. The room was
the same, unchanged in any way. I could see along the floor, in
some light without a source, my own footsteps in the dust. In
the light opposite me were three women. Even in the dream I
thought I had to be dreaming because the light was behind
them, and they threw no shadow. Two of the women were dark.
One was Bedelia Sue Frye in her vampire costume, and the
other was Camile Shatzkin in her widow's black dress. Their
eyes were dark and seemed almost red. The other woman was
blonde with great wavy golden hair and eyes like pale sap-
phires. I seemed somehow to know her face and couldn't remember how or where. All three had brilliant white teeth that
shone like pearls against the red of their soft lips. There was
something about them that made me uneasy, some longing and
at the same time some deadly fear. I felt in my chest a hope
that they would kiss me with those red lips. They whispered
together and laughed. It sounded like waterglasses tinkling.
The blonde girl shook her head and the other two urged her on.
Camile said:

"Go on. You're first and then us."

Bedelia continued, "He's strong. There are kisses for us
all."

The blonde girl came forward and I couldn't move,
couldn't call my father or brother. She bent over me till I could
feel her breath on me, honey-sweet and at the same time bitter.
Then I smelled blood and recognized her. It was Bedelia Sue
Frye as I had seen her in the early evening. She was two people
in the same room with me, and I was frightened.

She arched her neck and licked her lips like an animal till I could see the moisture shining on her lips and on the red tongue as it touched the white sharp teeth. Lower and lower went her head as her lips moved below the range of my mouth and chin and seemed to fasten on my throat. Then she paused, and I could hear the churning sound of her tongue as it licked her teeth and lips, and I could feel the skin of my throat begin to tingle the way your skin feels when you expect someone to tickle you. I could feel the soft, shivering touch of the lips on my throat and the hard dents of two sharp teeth, just touching and pausing there. I closed my eyes and waited. But something made a noise, and I opened them to see Bela Lugosi.

"Go, go," he shouted at the three women, taking his cigar out of his mouth to wave them from the basement. "I must awaken him, for there is work to be done."

And I woke up. My mattress was soaked with sweat.

"Toby," came a voice. I looked around and saw no one. Then I made out a face and figure.

"You screamed," said Gunther Wherthman, standing near my mattress on the floor.

"Nightmare," I told him, sitting up. "What time is it?"

"It is just after 6:30," he said, looking at the Beech-Nut gum clock.

I got up, flexed my good leg, and moved my sore knee to be sure it would work. Then I turned on the radio and listened to Fibber McGee and Molly for a while while Gunther volunteered to scramble a few eggs and make toast. Mayor LaTrivia tried to convince McGee to run for water commissioner against Gildersleeve, but McGee said he had his own fish to fry. I didn't say anything through the meal, and Gunther didn't ask me anything more. Things were coming together, and my mind was clearing. I poured some ketchup on the eggs and put them between two pieces of toast.

"I think I've got it," I said, taking a bite that left me about half a sandwich.

"You know who your murderer is?" Gunther asked politely, taking a small forkful of egg.

"Right," I said, chewing. "Now all I need is some evidence."

"Or a confession from the culprit? Is that an archaic word, 'culprit'?"

"It isn't used much in my circles," I said, finishing the sandwich.

I borrowed a couple of nickels from Gunther, got dressed, and called the murderer.

CHAPTER NINE

If you want to put things on an epic scale, fate intervened and stayed the course of the schedule I had set for the next few hours. If you want to put things in perspective, you simply say I had a flat tire, which is about ten minutes' work, since I had a spare. That is, it's ten minutes' work if you have a tire iron, which I did not. Mine was in the kitchen of an apartment in Culver City.

Mrs. Plaut had a car, a 1927 Ford that had remained untouched in her garage since 1928, the year Mr. Plaut died. I knew she had some tools in the garage with the car, and I hurried to get the key.

"I wonder if I could borrow some tools," I said after Mrs. Plaut opened her door and blessed me with a smile.

"They are, they are," she said with a wise, sad shake of her head and started to close the door on me. I had to put out my hand to stop her.

"My car," I shouted. "I need a tire iron." I mimed the changing of a tire and held her attention. "Tire iron. Tools."

"Fools?"

"Tools."

"Tools," she said finally in comprehension. "Out in the garage. I'll get the key."

Five minutes later I was changing the tire and trying not to get dirty. Time was shuffling away, singing a crazy old tune while I tried to catch up. The sun was still around when I finished and hurried in to wash my hands.

When I returned the keys to Mrs. Plaut, she took my sleeve and dragged me into her living room.

"You must listen to this part," she said. Mrs. Plaut had been writing her family history for the last ten years. It was over 1200 pages long, and whenever she could trap me or Gunther, she read it to us. She was under the impression that I was a part-time writer. I never found out where she got this impression.

"Mrs. Plaut," I said patiently, looking at my watch and getting pushed into her overstuffed chair. "I've got to go. It's a matter of life and death."

"Of course," she said, finding the pages on her oak table. "Here it is."

She showed me a page with an oblong box that looked like a coffin drawn on it.

"That's California," she explained.

"And those arrows pointing at it from each direction?" I asked.

"One on the left is England. Sir Francis Drake claimed California for Queen Elizabeth. One on top is Russia. They were after California. One on the right is France. They had the land the other side of the Rockies. The one below is Spain coming up from Mexico. Those poor damned Indians didn't know what hit them."

"But if this is your family history," I asked reasonably, "why are you giving California's . . ."

"Context," she said with satisfaction. "Got to know what we came to. History of turmoil."

"Terrific," I said, getting up with difficulty and barely

escaping the plate of cookies she held waist-high. "Leave it in my room. I'll look at it when I get back."

I went out the door and into the street without looking back. Seconds later, I was on my way to the St. Bartholomew Library. It was a few minutes after seven when I got there, and the same crust of a librarian watched my arrival with erect superiority. My footsteps echoed through St. Bart's, and I wondered whether Clinton Hill was still burrowed below our feet in some dark clanking corner.

"Your name is not Chadwick," the librarian said with lofty superiority. "And I do not believe you have academic credentials."

"Right," I said. "But it doesn't matter if I'm Albert Einstein or St. Bartholomew; you've got my gun and I want it. Now."

"I told you, we will not be . . ."

"I've got a flashlight," I said. "And I'll look for it myself."

"As you wish," he said uncomfortably. "You have twenty minutes and you must be quiet. And find it or not, I would like you to leave the library and never return. You can leave your real name and address, and we will return your firearm to you if you do not locate it."

"Fair is fair," I said, heading for the spiral staircase.

A girl with short hair and glasses at one of the tables looked up at me from a thick book as I passed. Her hand was in her hair, and she looked as if the very binding of the book confused her.

On the second level down, I pulled the flashlight from my back pocket and found a ladder leading into the pitch blackness below. I started down and got about ten feet when I heard a sound above me and I looked up. I could make out an outline. Then the outline laughed, a laugh that shook the ladder.

"Hill?" I said.

"It's not there," he said. "Your gun's not there. I've got it. See?"

I turned the flashlight up and saw my gun staring down at me.

"Thanks," I said, climbing back upward and trying to ignore the fact that he wasn't holding it in a way that looked like the offer of a friend.

"You almost got me fired," he said, still pointing the gun down at me.

"I didn't tell that guy to jump me here," I said, taking another rung up. "Put the gun down. What are you going to do? Shoot me for almost losing you your job? You want to lose your job, just go around shooting people."

He backed away slightly, and I came up over the railing very slowly.

"You've told the Dark Knights about me, haven't you?" he said, still pointing the gun in my direction.

"No, and I don't plan to," I said. "The fastest way out of the Dark Knights is to shoot me."

"You'd tumble over the rail and go into the darkness," he mused. "I could hide you."

I counted on Wilson Wong's assessment of Clinton Hill and took another step forward.

"Your hand is shaking, for Chrissake," I said. "Clinton, you aren't going to shoot anyone but yourself. You'll blast your foot off."

He handed me the gun meekly and laughed again.

"Would that I were made of sterner stuff," he sighed.

"Would that you were," I said, checking to be sure the gun was still loaded and working. As far as I could tell, it was. "Why not get out in the sun for a while?"

"The sun," he said hoarsely, "can kill you."

"You're not a vampire," I reminded him.

"I know," he said, "but I am human. The sun can give you cancer of the skin."

"You're a hell of a conversationalist, Clinton," I said, pocketing the gun.

"You're really not going to tell them?" he asked softly.

"Cross my heart and hope to die," I said and started upward.

The librarian with the tight collar was waiting for me at the top of the staircase.

"You made noise again," he observed.

"Right," I said. "I found the Frankenstein monster under all those papers and it gave me quite a start."

"I do not find your attempts at levity amusing," the librarian said, following me to the door and looking for bulges in case I had heisted a rare third edition of the Gutenberg Bible.

"Sorry," I said, "I do better when I'm not worried about getting killed."

The librarian could make nothing of me and went back to his counter, while I hurried to my car. The radio told me Mac-Arthur was making a desperate stand on Bataan, Roosevelt was calling for a $59 billion war budget, and Mickey Rooney and Ava Gardner had been married. I turned off the news and listened to Eddie Cantor till I got to Levy's restaurant on Sprina. Carmen was there behind the cash register, explaining a check to a couple. The man couldn't understand why he was being charged for the barley soup, which he thought came with the meal. Carmen patiently explained that the soup was extra. He raved a while longer, and she gave me a resigned shrug and then repeated her explanation.

The guy turned to me. His face was red with rage. He was a little guy, a head shorter than his wife, but it was clear he was the boss. "Any other restaurant, the soup comes with the meal."

"It's the war," I explained. "We all have to do our part."

"Maybe you're right," the man said a bit sheepishly. What he should have said was, What the hell has that got to do with anything, but patriotism was running high and with the Japanese bragging that they could invade California whenever they wanted, all it took was a hint that someone was less than

patriotic and he'd be surrounded by uglies and acidic old
ladies.

"I'll pay for my soup and pay gladly," I said.

The guy paid his bill and yanked his wife out of the restaurant.

"Well," said Carmen, looking at me for an explanation of
what I wanted and where I had been. Widowhood stood well
on Carmen. She could give Camile Shatzkin a few lessons.

"I've been working," I said. "Two cases. Long hours, usual
pay. How about that movie and dinner tomorrow?"

"No nightclub?" she said in mock disappointment.

"That was a combination of business and pleasure."

"The Chocolate Soldier with Nelson Eddy's at the Chinese
Loew's State," she said, leaning toward me with a smile.

"Tomorrow," I said. "My corner of the world will be back
in one piece by tomorrow." I could have added that it would
either be in one piece, or I wouldn't be part of it.

"Tomorrow," she agreed. "I'm off all afternoon and
night."

I took her hand, gave it a loud kiss that caused heads to
turn, and ordered a corned beef on rye with ketchup to go. It's
hard to be romantic in a kosher restaurant. While I waited, I
called Lugosi's house. He was home. I told him I expected his
problem to be over by morning and that I was going to see
Billings.

I got the sandwich, chucked it under my arm, bid adieu to
Carmen, and went out to meet my fate or my maker.

A second call to my murderer resulted in no answer, which
concerned me. I had called a few hours earlier and said I was
coming over to talk about something related to the Shatzkin
murder. The murderer had promised to be home from ten
o'clock on. I still had time to wrap up one of my cases before
then, so I headed into Los Angeles to do it. By now I knew the
way.

When I got where I was going, the sun was down, and the sky was rumbling with the threat of rain. What made it worse was the general blackout. There wasn't much to see.

I parked next to the theater and walked up to the box office. It was closed and the theater was dark. I tried the doors. None were open.

Moving around the side of the building just as the first few drops fell, I found a house behind the theater on top of a little hill. It was an old three-story frame house that had once been white, but time and inattention had turned it gray. There was no light, but I walked up the hill on my still aching leg and climbed the steps. They creaked mightily and the sound mixed with the whirl of the rainy wind.

The porch held an old swing that rocked gently back and forth in the wind as if someone were sitting in it. I knocked. No one answered. I knocked again. Still no answer. My next step was to pull the flashlight out of my pocket and hit the windows with its beam. The place looked empty. I backed off the porch into the rain and shined the light on the second floor. I thought I caught one of the curtains fluttering, but I couldn't be sure. Whistling an invented tune, I went back on the porch and tried the door. It opened with a perfect creak of hinges that would have sent the Three Stooges scrambling out into the downpour.

My flashlight beam hit a stairway and several rooms. From what I could see in the fading beam, it was decorated in early Lizzie Borden.

"Billings," I called. No answer. I thought I heard something above me.

"Come on, Sam," I called, pointing my beam up the stair. "Just take out your fangs and let's talk. I've got a lot to do tonight."

Again something creaked above. My yellow light went dim, and I turned what was left of it to the walls, in search of a light switch. I found it and flicked it, but nothing happened.

My flashlight decided it had done enough for one Eveready lifetime and closed its eye. Outside, the rain was coming down hard, heavy, and tired. A little lightning joined it, and I reached for my gun. My eyes began to adjust to the liquid gloom in a few seconds, during which I held my gun ready. When I could see a little, I put the gun back in the holster.

"Sam," I sighed falsely, "you are being difficult."

The dank smell of the house caught me with a touch of nausea as I put my foot on the first step. Above, in the flashes of lightning, I could make out the top of the stairway. I went up slowly, my back sliding against the wall, my knee counting each step in pain.

It only took me four or five days to get to the landing where I was sure Billings would leap out at me with artificial fangs and either go for my neck or offer me a Hires Root Beer. He didn't, and I resigned myself to hide and seek. I remembered a "Suspense" episode with Ralph Edwards in which he played a scoffing radio reporter who spends a night in a haunted house and goes crazy. It was not a good thing to remember, but one has little control over such things. I tried to think that MacArthur had it worse on Bataan, but that didn't help. I couldn't believe in Bataan. It didn't really exist. What did exist was this matchstick house and my fear.

"Billings," I shouted. "I'm getting angry."

The hall light switch didn't work either. The storm had knocked off the power, or maybe the place just didn't have any power. Or maybe someone had pulled some fuses.

Bedrooms lined the hall wall, and each one seemed to be empty when I opened the door. None of them looked lived in. At the end of the hall was a balcony looking down on the living room. I stepped on the balcony and waited till the lightning cut cold light and showed me nothing. I heard another movement, higher above. I turned and found the stairway in front of me going up to what I assumed was the last floor of Billings's manor.

"Sam," I said, "this is aggravating a sore knee, and you

have nowhere to go. Sooner or later, this game will be over."

I moved up. These stairs were even narrower than the ones below. When I got to the landing, I thought I could hear someone breathing. The three doors on the floor looked as if they were closed. I moved to the first one, kicking it open. Nothing.

Below I thought I heard something, a slight creak, and then I was sure. Someone was opening the front door and being announced by the musical hinges.

"Who's down there?" I yelled, stepping back into the hall. No one answered. I stopped, trying not to breathe, but that proved to be too much to ask of a sorely tried soul.

I thought I heard the creak of stairs. I moved to the stairwell and leaned over. I couldn't see anything. The lightning chose that moment to penetrate the house with a crack of light, and my eyes caught a shadow on the stairs.

"Far enough," I said. "I've got a gun."

The answer to my threat was a pinging near my head. The shot had missed me by what seemed not at all. I pulled out my .38 and aimed down the stairs.

It was a good time to break my record of never having shot anyone. I leaned forward, took aim, and fired. Something moved out of the room behind me, and I turned to meet it. Whatever it was jostled me, and I tried to keep from tumbling head first over the railing and down the stairs. I could hear the figure who bumped into me scrambling for a dark hole, and I could feel the gun fly out of my hand while I desperately grabbed for something to hold onto. The stairway had been narrow enough so my hand caught the far side, and I pushed myself back. My .38 hit the wooden stairs and thumped six or seven steps.

Silence. I was breathing hard and licking sweat from my upper lip, trying to see below, to see whether I had a chance at my gun before whoever was coming up and shooting at me got to it first. I didn't even worry about who or what had been behind me.

There was no lightning, and I could see no gun below, but I could hear the footsteps coming slowly, carefully upward. In a few seconds, maybe thirty or forty at most, whoever was on the way up would probably find my gun and know I was unarmed. Even if they didn't find it, they'd figure out that I had stopped firing back. What I needed was a weapon. Since this was Sam Billings's house, I doubted that I'd even find a heavy crucifix to throw, but what choice did I have? Don't bother to answer. It's always easier to find options when the knife is at someone else's throat.

I slipped off my shoes and carried them into the first room. There was a table in the corner and something that looked like a bench. I groped my way to the table, and my hand touched something erect and smooth. It was a candle. I moved to the wall, running my hand across it. Nothing. Below me the footsteps were moving upward. I hadn't counted the steps, but I knew they weren't infinite. A chair could be a weapon, but that would be a last resort against someone with a gun. The footsteps were moving up rapidly. It was time for last resorts. I grabbed a chair, almost losing it in my sweating hands, and placed my shoes on the table. I moved behind the door and waited and waited and waited. The stairs creaked, and the wind blew, and the rain fell, and I thought I was going to be sick. The trick would be to swing the chair just when the person with the gun stepped in. The chair was getting heavy and I was fighting an almost uncontrollable urge to giggle in fright.

My sensitivity shell was alive with nerves. I could hear a thousand aches and sighs in the building. My brain tried to sort them out, determine which was the right one. I thought I caught a creak on the floor outside and tried to tighten my grip, but I didn't want to make noise. Now, I thought, but another voice inside said, wait. I waited, waited, waited, and when I couldn't take another surge of my pulse, I stepped out and swung the chair. I hit something and heard a pained "Urrgg."

Dropping the chair, I took a step into the hall to throw a

kick, which would not have been devastating in my bare feet, but it beat trying to run or hide. The barrel of a gun jabbed my chest, and I stopped suddenly. My stockinged feet slid, and I was on my back in the room, which saved me from getting the bullet in the chest. I rolled back and kicked the door closed, but another bullet came through the wood close enough to make my right ear ring.

What could I do? I backed away. The door opened slowly, and I could see enough to know that I was in a room with the murderer I had been looking for. My idea had been to set the scene, but the murderer had decided not to wait.

The gun picked me out but didn't fire. I watched while the murderer kept me in sight and groped to the table. I was motioned away by the dark outline, and I moved away. The sounds told me that there was something being pulled out of a pocket, and the striking of a match told me what it was. The murderer lit the candle and turned to face me.

CHAPTER TEN

The light from the single candle revealed a small room. I was near the door. To my right was a blank wall with three old glass-covered oval photographs on it, all of women about fifty. The wall to my left was covered from ceiling to floor with heavy, blood-red drapes. I had seen curtains like this before, in the basement of the theater a few dozen yards away where the Dark Knights had met. That seemed a long time ago. But it had been only five days. On the wall opposite me was a single window, small, dirty, and crying with rain. There were a few chairs, and the one table with a cloth. On the table was a statue of some kind with a bunch of arms. Oh, in front of the table stood Jerry Vernoff, aiming a gun in my general direction.

"I know we were supposed to meet at my place later," he said, leaning back against the table. He was dripping with rain and his yellow hair was plastered forward on his brow. "But I started to think that you had no reason to see me and maybe, just maybe you were putting things together. I can tell by your eyes that you're not surprised to see me, so I can also conclude that I was right. Pretty good, huh?"

"Third rate," I said, slumped back against the wall. His face sagged, and his grip tightened on the gun. I had hit home. He wanted to shoot, but he wanted to hear more. I hoped I had read this whole thing and him right and that Vernoff would want to talk about it.

"Third rate?" he said irritably. "Come on. The plotting was . . ."

". . . too complicated," I finished. He reached over and threw me my shoes. I figured he wouldn't shoot until I got them on, and by that time we'd be deep in debate, and I might get to do something. He was about ten feet away, so there wasn't much chance to go for him. My best bet would probably be to catch him off guard in the middle of a sentence and try to go out the door and down the stairs. I didn't know how well my knee would do with that option, and a fleeting sense of morbid satisfaction took me. If Vernoff shot me in the back before I made it down the stairs, it would be Phil's fault for mashing my knee. Then he wouldn't be singing, "I'll be glad when you're dead, you rascal you."

"What do you mean, too complicated?" Vernoff pressed.

I stood up and looked around as if I had the duration of the war to while away.

"The Shatzkin murder," I said. "Why not just shoot him and say a burglar did it? That's what started me thinking about you. Each murder, Shatzkin's, Newcomb's, Haliburton's, had a gimmick, a B-movie plot gimmick, your specialty."

Vernoff was hurting, and my words were giving him head troubles.

"We handed the police a wrapped-up murderer for Shatz-kin," Vernoff said.

"We? You mean you and Mrs. Shatzkin? How about New-comb and Haliburton?"

"Camile and I and Newcomb, but not Haliburton," Vernoff explained. "He never knew what was going on. He was just a big puppy dog who found out too much."

"A very active puppy dog," I said. Vernoff flared with jealousy.

"What do you mean?"

"Come on, Jerry," I said. "You've got the plot in your files. Good-looking hulk like Haliburton. You think your roving Camile never dallied in the garden?"

"She was just stringing him along, using him," Vernoff explained.

"You're giving me B dialogue again, Jerry," I said.

"And I can blow a hole right through . . ." he stopped.

"More B dialogue," I said, pointing out what he had already noticed. "That's your problem."

"I can write," Vernoff said. "Now that Camile and I are going to have money, control of a big agency, I'll get the ins, the breaks. That's all you need, good connections. Talent isn't enough."

"I think Warner Baxter said that in *42nd Street,*" I pushed.

"That's enough, Peters," he shouted, and I could see it was enough. I went in another direction. "You met Camile Shatzkin while you were her husband's client?"

"Right," he said, calming down a bit. "A party at his place. I talked to her for a while. She was interested in my work, my career. One thing led to another, and she said she wanted to read some of my material. I invited her to drop by whenever she wanted to. Then it started."

"You think she was already planning to use you to get rid of her husband?" I said.

"That was my idea. It was all my idea." He pointed to himself with his left thumb, and I could see that Jerry Vernoff was losing control. He didn't want to be told he was a character and Camile Shatzkin was the author.

"I got the idea for getting rid of Shatzkin right out of my files," he said proudly. "Thayer Newcomb was an old acquaintance who, like me, had never had a break. He was a good actor, but he had a reputation for doing wild things, violence. He called Shatzkin, said he was Faulkner, and made a lunch appointment for 1:30 on Wednesday. Then he called Faulkner, said he was Shatzkin, and made an appointment for noon on Wednesday. When Faulkner showed up in front of Shatzkin's office, Thayer was on the stairway, waiting. He came down and bumped into Faulkner as if he were on the way out of his office. He got Faulkner in a cab and over to Bernstein's restaurant. He did a good job."

"More B-picture stuff," I couldn't resist saying. "Newcomb didn't study his part. He played Shatzkin as a loud, fast-talking agent right out of Ned Sparks. That was one of the first things that made me suspicious. Shatzkin's secretary, a solid type, said her boss was anything but what Newcomb played for Faulkner."

"Well . . ." Vernoff said, off-balance.

"Let me go on," I said, inching, or quarter-inching, toward the door as I pretended to shift my weight. "He dumped Faulkner, promised to get back to him, and then went to the restaurant where he had made a reservation and date to meet Shatzkin. He put on a false mustache and played Faulkner, obviously doing a better job than he did as Shatzkin because he got a dinner invitation. Right?"

"Right," Vernoff beamed, remembering his triumph as author-director of the crime.

"Then," I continued, "Newcomb showed up at the Shatzkins' and shot innocent victim Jacques. Luckily for your plot, Shatzkin lived long enough to actually identify his assailant as Faulkner, the man he had invited to dinner and had lunch with. Camile was happy to support his identification. You forgot to account for how Camile could identify Faulkner, whom she never met. She positively identified a photo of Harry James as Faulkner."

"A slight error," Vernoff agreed, "but I took care of that."

"Sure you did," I said, doing some more inching. "She panicked and ran to meet you at your Culver City love nest, and when I found out about the place, she tried to protect you by saying Newcomb was her lover. More complications."

"I didn't panic," said Vernoff with self-approval.

"Not right away," I went on. "Instead you decided to try to buy some time. I had told you about my Bela Lugosi case, and you decided with Newcomb to try to get me to work on that, to throw a few scares into me to head me in the wrong direction. Newcomb's best acting jobs in this whole thing were his attacks on me."

"He wasn't just acting," Vernoff said, "I told you he was a violent man."

I said, "Why did you involve Faulkner in all this?"

"He was handy," Vernoff said defensively.

"And you didn't like him having the reputation you wanted," I pushed. "He was the big man, the famous writer."

"Maybe a little of that," Vernoff agreed. The candle sputtered from a breeze somewhere, and I tensed, ready to go for the door, but it stayed on, and I let my weight fall back against the wall. "Faulkner is a self-satisfied, superior . . . he didn't like me, made it clear that he thought I was a hack. I'll tell you, he needed me. He stinks with plots."

"So," I went on, "on Friday night when you were working with him, you played into his feelings, made yourself . . ."

"Obnoxious," Vernoff finished.

"Easy acting job," I said. Vernoff shook his head in mock pity at my lack of understanding. "You suggested the break just before nine, and Faulkner jumped at it and ran for a drink. That way you couldn't provide him with an alibi. But what if someone else did remember him?"

"I followed him, made sure. He came back to his room when he was sure I was gone. It was perfect."

The rain eased slightly, went to calm, and then exploded in anger with the biggest torrent of all.

"Okay, we jump back ahead," I said. "Newcomb is attacking me in parking lots and libraries. He calls Lugosi with a big threat—by the way, did he actually have to read that one line of telephone dialogue? He couldn't even remember it? I found it in his wallet."

"I wanted to be sure he delivered the exact line," Vernoff explained.

"Mistakes, mistakes, Jerry," I sighed. "Finding that card in his pocket, just like all the other cards in your apartment, gave me ideas. Why did you kill Newcomb?"

"It doesn't take much to figure it out," he said, shifting the gun in his hand to get a better grip. "Thayer and I followed you to that nightclub in Glendale and agreed simply to run you down and make it look like an accident. The police weren't after us. You were. With you gone, we'd be in the clear."

"Wrong," I said. "The police would have started going over the same steps, especially if I coincidentally got hit by a car."

"That's your opinion," he said testily. It was, but my opinion was based on experience, not daydreams.

"So you didn't kill me, and I came chasing you."

"Yes," said Vernoff, "and while I drove I started to think. Camile had suggested that Thayer was her lover. If Thayer died, you might be at a dead end, especially if his death looked like it was tied in to the Lugosi case. Besides, who knows when or whether Thayer might someday start thinking of blackmail or might get caught and say things I wouldn't like? I headed for the Culver City apartment. I parked near the apartment and shot him. Then I pushed the wooden stake into him to cover the bullet."

"Got rid of a lot with one blow," I said. "No need to give him a kickback and no need to worry about blackmail in the future."

"I knew what I was doing," he said proudly.

I shook my head and could see by the dancing candlelight in his eyes that he didn't appreciate my lack of appreciation.

"What was wrong?"

"Everything you did linked my two cases," I explained. "All I had to do was to go back over the list of people who knew I was on both cases. I had told you because of our discussion over beer about plot. And the whole thing just kept getting more and more plot-complicated. I tell you, Jerry, you would have been better off just blasting your victims, tossing the gun in the ocean, and going to work as usual. What about Haliburton?"

At some point before dawn, Vernoff's tale would be over, and he would decide to leave another corpse. I would have liked the door closer and my odds better, but I'd have to take what I could get.

"You got him going," Vernoff said. "You planted the idea in his mind that Camile might have been responsible for her husband's death and might have been friendly with Thayer."

"Which wasn't true?"

"Not about Thayer," said Vernoff. "I'm going to have to wrap this up, Peters. I don't know who owns this place, but they might be coming back and I don't want to be here."

"You followed me here?"

"Yes," he said. "You wanted to know about Haliburton. He heard Camile talking to me on the phone yesterday and confronted her, said he knew what had happened and was leaving. Camile called me and stalled him. She reached me a few minutes after I got back home from the Culver City apartment. I managed to get to Bel Air in time to follow Haliburton to the Hotel Belvedere."

"Where you checked in and played Mr. Mann, complete with a shaving cream mask. Where did you get the shotgun?"

"My father's. He hunts. I never could see the point in killing innocent animals you didn't plan to eat," he said.

"What about people?" I said. "Innocent ones like Haliburton?" And me for that matter, but I didn't say it.

"That was different," Vernoff said with emotion. "That was survival. Him or me."

"And Shatzkin? Was that survival, too? Your father will be proud of you when he hears about your hunting trip. Bagged three big ones, dad, all human."

"Four," Vernoff grinned. "You forgot yourself."

"Why stop there?" I said "Why not kill Faulkner? He might start coming up with more details about his meeting with the fake Shatzkin. Or Camile? She hasn't been a model of discretion. Why not Lugosi? There's no end to the possible victims an enterprising writer with a distorted imagination can come up with."

"That's enough," he said.

But I was going now. Survival was important, and I might get Vernoff angry now that I was running out of tales to swap with him, but I was angry too. I didn't want to be lost in the list of victims in a plot right out of Vernoff's card file.

"Jerry, you didn't do anything right," I said.

"Well, we'll just have to see if I can learn from my mistakes from this point on," he said, raising the gun in my direction. There was just about no chance that I could make it to the door without his getting a shot off, but he might miss, or he might not hit me someplace that would slow me down, or he might not . . . the time for guessing and thinking was over.

There was a creaking, something like the hinges of the front door. The sound came from behind the red-draped wall. Both Vernoff and I looked at the billowing drapes as the candle flickered. Vernoff's gun turned toward the drapes, which parted. Dracula stepped out. He was in his familiar tuxedo and cape. He pulled the cape over his face to cover his nose and mouth. His eyes burned into Vernoff, and his long right hand rose and pointed a pale finger at the man holding the gun.

"Put down the gun," he commanded. "Put *it* down."

Vernoff fired wildly, his eyes wide. The shot went some-where into the ceiling, and I scrambled forward at him before he could recover. I got him around the waist but couldn't bring him down. He was a big man, but I was holding on for my life. He hit my back with the gun, and I punched at his groin. He let out a groan and doubled over. The gun clattered into a dark corner. On my back with a burning shoulder, I saw Vernoff looking at the figure of Dracula moving slowly toward him. In spite of his pain, Vernoff went for the door. He wasn't moving fast, but I was having trouble moving at all. My gun was out there somewhere and he might find it, pull himself together, and realize he had to finish what he'd started.

I followed him out the door, moving past Dracula, who stood motionless. Vernoff was at the top few steps with his hand to his groin, where I had hit him. It was dark, but I could see him hunched over like Quasimodo. I went over the rail and onto his back, and we tumbled down the narrow stairs. It had happened to me before and I knew what to do. My arms held him tightly, and I curled my head in. He took most of the bumps. When we hit the landing on the second floor, I let go and Vernoff hit the wall with a thud.

He seemed to be through, but I wasn't in the mood for much more. That would have been the end if my eye hadn't caught my gun no more than a short reach from his hand. He started to rise, and I tried but wasn't sure I could. Then the crack of lightning hit close, sending flashbulb brightness. Vernoff saw the gun and started to bend for it, but he paused to turn to the creak on the stairs above.

Dracula was bathed in another lightning flash, and his voice rose above it in a warning, "STOP."

Vernoff backed away, caught himself, and went for the gun. I pushed myself forward, and my head drove into his head. The crack sent a shock from my skull through the big toe on my right foot. Vernoff, his skull less experienced in pain, staggered back with a groan. He hit something in the dark that creaked and cracked, and then his outline disappeared.

My hand was on the wall to steady me, and another hand held me up.

"Where did he go?" I asked, my head dancing colors before my eyes.

"He fell tnrough the railing on the balcony," Lugosi's voice came at my side.

He helped me to the railing, which had a gap where Vernoff had gone through. Looking down, we could see his shape in the living room. He wasn't moving.

"It was an effective performance?" Lugosi asked.

"It saved my life," I said.

In the next crack of lightning I could see a small smile of satisfaction on the actor's face.

My rest was brief. There was a definite movement above us, and it wasn't rats. It was footsteps, and I remembered the figure that had bumped into me when the shooting started.

CHAPTER ELEVEN

My gun was in my hand, and my senses were returning to near normal, which meant that I could see, hear, and feel about as well as the average living Civil War veteran.

I went back up the stairs with Lugosi following. This time I went slowly, not because of fear, but because of an aching body.

"Go downstairs, call the cops. Get the Wilshire District. Ask for Lieutenant Pevsner or Sergent Seidman," I said. "If Vernoff's not dead, get an ambulance. And see if you can find the fuse box and get the lights on."

"Yes," said Lugosi, and he swept down the stairs with his cape billowing.

I went up, not trying to be quiet. The candle was still on. It guided me. I went into the room, picked it up, and found Vernoff's gun.

"Billings," I shouted. "I'm in no mood for this. Get your ass out here. If I have to find you . . ."

Something scrambled above my head. I went into the hall and found a wooden ladder to what looked like a loft.

"Billings," I shouted up into the darkness. "I don't want to climb this thing. I've got a game knee. Stop sucking your thumb and get down here."

Something shuffled and moved above and stopped.

"Would a couple of bullets up there help make up your mind?" I asked.

The trap door opened. I could hear it, but I couldn't see anything. Billings's voice came down in a high quaver.

"What do you want?"

"There's a corpse in your living room," I said sweetly. "And we have some things to talk about."

"How do I know you won't hurt me?" he said.

"Cross my heart," I said. "I promise. Will you just get down here before the cops come? If I have to climb up there in my present condition and state of mind, our conversation will be far less pleasant than . . ."

The lights went on. The place was not exactly lit like a sound stage, but it was lit, and I could see Billings's pale face. He started to draw back into his hole and I shouted, "Oh no, ease your belly down here, Count."

He came down slowly, sheepishly, heavily. He was wearing his vampire costume, and he looked frightened. He had reason to be.

"Let's go downstairs," I said, letting him lead the way. I blew out the candle and put it on the landing.

"I didn't . . ." he began on the second floor when he saw his broken railing.

"Yes, you did," I said, prodding him gently with my hand. The point on my back where Vernoff had hit me was throbbing violently.

On the main floor, Billings tried to turn toward the rear of the house, but I guided him into the living room. Vernoff was lying there, his eyes open, staring at his hand, which would type no more of the plots his smashed skull could not deliver. Billings tried not to look at the corpse, but he was fascinated and finally fixed his eyes on it.

"That's what a real dead one looks like, Count," I said. "Does it get you all excited? Ah, ah, no running for the toilet. You're a great big vampire, aren't you? You were going to put the fear of heaven and hell into Bela Lugosi with your threats."

"How did you know it was me?" he said, his eyes still fixed on Vernoff's body.

"Sam," I said. "I've got a blow for you. You are the only member of the Dark Knights who takes the thing seriously. The others have their own hobby horses. Riding Lugosi was yours. I'd like to know why."

Billings forced his eyes away from Vernoff and roamed the room. I followed him and realized that I had seen the place somewhere before. I was getting that feeling a lot.

"This is Dr. Seward's living room." he said softly. "His office is next door."

Lugosi appeared at the door behind Billings. He was about to speak, but his eyes too scanned the room in recognition.

"It's exactly like the rooms in *Dracula,*" Billings said. "That was more than a movie for me. It was a possibility, a possibility that couldn't be betrayed. Don't you see? I couldn't let Lugosi, the real Count, sink to ridicule."

Billings still did not see Lugosi, who watched from the door and listened.

"You see," continued Billings, "he is not a real vampire, but an inspiration to those of us who are."

"You're a real vampire?" I said.

Billings nodded in confession.

"You have a coffin you sleep in and the whole works?" I said in disbelief.

"Yes," said Billings. "In the cellar."

"Have you ever . . ." I began. "I mean blood."

"Not yet," he said seriously. "But soon."

Lugosi took a step into the room, and Billings turned toward him with a gasp.

"Mr. Billings," Lugosi said gently. "Neither you nor I are vampires. We are simply men with dreams that do not come true and with which we must learn to live."

"No," said Billings defiantly. His next *no* was less defiant and more to a voice within him than to Lugosi or to me. Finally, he looked at Vernoff's corpse and sank into a chair with his eyes closed.

"The police will be here momentarily," Lugosi said. "I fear your Mr. Wernhoff is dead."

I looked at Lugosi with curiosity through my pain, and he looked down at his costume and gave a smile of understanding.

"Tonight I am to appear at a screening of *Dracula* at an Army benefit performance. I have a little act taken from my stage role as Dracula which I can do. It's not much, but it goes nicely with the picture. You told me you were coming here, and you sounded troubled, so I came in a cab. I found the theater closed and came to the house. The door was opened, and I heard your voice and Mr. Wernhoff's above. I came up and saw him with the gun on you, so I moved into the next room, where I found the door leading to the room you were in. I listened and tried to time my entrance so that it would be most effective and beneficial."

"So," I said, "you heard some of what he said?"

"Enough to know he killed some people," sighed Lugosi. "And this poor fellow," he said looking at Billings, "is the one who sent me those notes and the dead bat?"

"All except that last call, the death threat; that was the work of our friend on the floor. It was just to get me going in the wrong direction."

"Yes," sighed Lugosi. "Again I have been the red herring."

"In a way," I said, wobbling.

"Forgive me," said Lugosi, helping me to a chair and fishing out a cigar.

The three of us sat in silence, watching Vernoff's corpse, for about twenty minutes. Lugosi, his cape draped over the back of his chair, smoked and threw an occasional look of pity or concern at Billings, who couldn't bring himself to meet Lugosi's eyes.

When Phil came in followed by Seidman, we probably looked like a quartet of corpses.

"What the hell is this?" Phil said in that combination of amazement and anger that was his alone. It meant, What has the force of evil come up with this time to make my life a walking hell.

"Guy on the floor is Vernoff," I said.

The name rang a bell.

"The one who couldn't give Faulkner an alibi?" said Phil.

"He didn't want to," I said. "He killed Shatzkin, Newcomb, and Haliburton. He was in it with Mrs. Shatzkin. He told me, and I have a reliable witness, Mr. Lugosi."

Lugosi looked up and waved his cigar in greeting.

Phil didn't know what to say to the familiar figure dressed like a vampire. I also realized that Phil had recognized the room but couldn't place it. Seidman simply looked tired.

"This isn't our jurisdiction," said Seidman.

"It's your case," I said.

"Who's that?" said Phil, pointing at Billings.

"It's his house," I explained.

"What has he got to do with this and why is he dressed like that?" Phil bubbled, his rage and confusion ready to burst red.

"It's a long story," I said, and I began to tell it while Seidman took my statement. I talked slowly but didn't have to. Seidman knew shorthand. The slow tale was for the benefit of the rest of us.

Lugosi followed with his part, playing it with flourishes and enjoyment.

We all looked at the corpse some more while Seidman found the phone and called for someone to take care of Vernoff and Billings. Phil looked as if he wanted to throw a couple of kicks at Vernoff and might have done it if the rest of us weren't there. I was clearly in agony from the blow to my back, my knee, and my roll down the stairs, and Lugosi was too old and well known to be hit. That left Billings, and I could see Phil savoring the possibility of a hard right to the soft figure. I watched desire rise in my brother's eyes, the wish to hit something solid, but Billings wasn't solid, and Phil gave up the desire and sat boiling.

Cawelti was the next one through the door. He spotted me and Phil and hesitated. He looked at Vernoff and Billings and didn't know what to do. Seidman handed him his notebook as two uniformed police came in behind him.

"My notes will explain," he said to Cawelti. "Get Mr. Lugosi wherever he wants to go and get this cleaned up."

Cawelti considered a question or protest, but Phil, looking for a victim, caught his eye, and he shut up.

"Come on," Phil said to me, pushing himself from the chair.

I got up and so did Lugosi. I took Lugosi's frail hand and shook it.

"Thanks for saving my life," I said.

"And thank you for a most interesting interlude," he said. "Please send me your bill for services."

"Right," I said and followed Seidman and Phil into the night. The rain had turned to drizzle. I knew where we were going.

"Can you drive?" Seidman asked.

I told him I could and went to my own car. We drove in tandem through Los Angeles. I caught part of a boxing match on the radio to keep me company, but I couldn't keep my mind on it long enough to know who was fighting or winning. The patter of the announcer and his false rise in excitement as he described the blows was like a friend at your side who jabbers on and you don't listen to, but you like having him there.

When we got to Bel Air, no one tried to stop us. The move up Chalon was getting routine for me, so I pulled ahead of Phil and Seidman and led the way.

The Shatzkin house was dark except for an upstairs light.

Phil was about to ham-hand the door when I put out my hand to stop him. He wheeled, ready to take my head, and then waited. I knocked gently. Then I knocked a little louder. In a while footsteps came down the stairs inside.

"Who is it?" came Camile Shatzkin's voice.

"Jerry," I said.

"Jerry?"

She fumbled with the door and kept talking. There was a touch of shrewish anger seething in her tone that Jerry Vernoff would never have the chance to be disillusioned by.

"I thought you were going to stay away from here," she hissed. "What happened? Did Peters . . ."

And the door flew open on the bright trio of Peters, Pevsner, and Seidman, a group that could have wilted an innocent person, let alone one as guilty as Camile Shatzkin.

"Trick or treat," I said.

She almost fainted, but Seidman moved forward to keep her from falling.

"I thought it was a delivery I was expecting," she said, pulling herself together.

"Do you usually faint when the delivery man comes?" I said.

Phil grabbed my arm and squeezed hard enough to let me know he wanted me to shut up.

Camile Shatzkin, in glimmering red robe, her dark hair down, looked every inch the opera star in her big moment.

"I've been under a great strain," she explained, pulling herself away from Seidman's support.

"That 'great strain' business might carry you about a week," I said. "Then you'll have to think up another line."

"Why are you here?" she demanded.

"Do you want to invite us in, or do you want to get dressed right now and come with us?" Phil asked wearily.

Camile Shatzkin flushed in indignation. We all expected her to say, "How dare you talk to me like that?" but she disappointed us by letting her nostrils flare in anger and stepping back to usher us into the living room. We'd been there before. We weren't impressed.

Mrs. Shatzkin sat down on a sofa after flipping on some lights and folded her hands in her lap, ready for anything. She looked at me briefly, trying to read some answers in my face, but my face doesn't hold any answers. My face is a weary question mark. I was willing to stare her down. The advantage was mine. She was easier to look at than I was, and I could read her with no trouble.

"Jerry Vernoff has confessed before two reliable witnesses that he killed your husband, Thayer Newcomb, and Haliburton," said Seidman. "He also said that you conspired with him to commit those murders."

I sat down without taking my eyes from Camile Shatzkin, and Phil looked around the room feigning boredom, acting as if this was the routine part of a case already wrapped up. There was nothing to read in Seidman's voice or face. He was simply giving information and withholding some. He didn't tell her that Vernoff was dead and probably in the morgue by now. He didn't tell her that all she had to do was say nothing to stay out of this, to walk away clean with her estate. There was no case on her, just the accusation of a dead man, a murderer three times over.

"How could he say such a thing?" she said, trembling. "I don't believe he . . . I think you're lying. And I think I'll have to ask you to leave and talk to my lawyer."

"I guess we'll have to book her and take her downtown," Phil said, examining a painting of a French landscape on the wall.

Camile Shatzkin said nothing.

"He's dead," I shot in.

Phil's head turned in my direction and Seidman shook his head.

Mrs. Shatzkin looked at me, but nothing dawned. Almost all the "he's" in her life were dead. I had to be more specific.

"Jerry Vernoff," I said. "He's dead. His neck is broken and he's lying in the morgue by now. One more on the slab and you'll have killed a whole basketball team worth of men."

"Jerry is . . .?" She smiled with a touch of madness and a shake of her head. "No. This is another trick."

"No trick," said Seidman, going along because there was nothing else to do. Phil was at my side. I hoped he wouldn't hit me in my sore back if he decided to strike. But he sensed a crack in Camile Shatzkin and stood waiting.

"Look," said Phil, "what're we bothering with this for? We have a man's dying confession and testimony. That's enough to hang her. If she wants to shut up, let her shut up."

Phil clearly had a way with words. We all looked down at Camile the Widow and waited to see which way she would go. If she told Phil to go chew on an electric eel, that was the end of it. If there was a clock ticking you could have heard it, but there wasn't. Luckily no one's stomach growled.

"I loved him," she said very quietly.

"What?" growled Phil.

Camile Shatzkin looked up with tears starting in her eyes. "I loved him."

"Jerry Vernoff?" Seidman said.

"Darryl," she said.

"Darryl?" said Phil, looking at me and Seidman. "Who the hell is Darryl?"

"Darryl Haliburton," she said, her eyes red. "I didn't know he was going to kill Darryl. I didn't really realize how much I loved him, needed him."

"Vernoff said it was your idea to get rid of your husband," said Seidman.

"It was his," she said, pulling a handkerchief from her robe. Her chest rose with a sob.

"How did you help?" I asked.

This was it, but she didn't know it.

"I didn't have to do anything, just let Newcomb in, watch him shoot Jacques, and make no effort to follow him. All I had to do was identify William Faulkner as the murderer."

"That lets my man off the hook?" I asked.

Phil nodded.

Seidman went upstairs with Mrs. Shatzkin to check her room and be sure there were no weapons of self- or other destructiveness. While she dressed, Phil and I sat in the living room ignoring each other.

"My knee's getting better," I said, sitting down.

Phil grunted. That was our conversation for the night.

CHAPTER TWELVE

I n which a famed writer returns home and this obscure private detective finds that financial security is hard to come by even in the best of times.

It was well after two in the morning when Faulkner was released. I was surprised that I wasn't particularly sleepy, though I was tired. I had been working a lot of nights since the two cases began. Faulkner looked composed, though I detected below that wry, thin exterior a tight sheet of controlled anger. He accepted his belongings and, to give him credit, didn't give the usual line about suing the Los Angeles Police Department for false arrest.

"Can I give you a ride back to your hotel?" I asked him, trying to reach the spot on my back where Vernoff had clobbered me with his gun.

Faulkner accepted and on the way sat looking out the window listening silently and pulling at his pipe while I told him the tale.

"That Vernoff should bear such rancor toward me suggests the frightening prospect of others who might harbor such thoughts about each of us without our knowing," he whispered.

Most of my enemies weren't so subtle, but I just nodded in

agreement. We paused at a red light and watched a drunk in a doorway trying to stand up and having a hell of a time at it. Faulkner and I both urged him up silently, and I forgot to move when the light went green. A kid in the car behind hit his horn and pulled me up to what passed for reality.

"I have informed Mr. Leib that I will repay him for the advance he gave you," Faulkner said, still not looking at me. "I would appreciate it if you would submit to me in Oxford the remainder of your bill. I do not wish to have any obligation to Warner Brothers or Mr. Leib."

"Fine," I said.

"It may be several weeks or longer till I can forward the amount," Faulkner continued in what was obviously a difficult statement, "but it will be forthcoming." He laughed without humor. "I have been writing for years about honor, truth, pity, consideration, and the capacity to endure grief and misfortune and injustice and then endure again, in terms of individuals who observed and adhered to such principles not for reward but for virtue's own sake in order to live with oneself and die peacefully with oneself, but there's no denying the needs of the body. Romantic virtue is constantly preyed upon by our animalism."

"Makes sense to me," I lied. "You're not sticking around Los Angeles, then?" I hurriedly changed the subject.

"No," he sighed. "I will leave my agent to try to negotiate something here. I'm needed in Oxford. I'm the area chief for the local aircraft warning system, though I can see little chance or reason for an air attack on the hinterlands of Mississippi. I've actually got an office over a drug store where I can recruit observers. My daughter Jill likes it. She's always complaining that she doesn't know what to indicate on school forms that ask what her daddy does. She thinks I don't work, but now she can list me as an air-raid warden."

"It's something," I said, turning down the block in front of the Hollywood Hotel.

Faulkner reached over to shake my hand when we stopped in front of the hotel. I hadn't been to the Hollywood for years and didn't realize how fast it had fallen to just this side of Gothic decay.

"If something ever brings you to Mississippi, Mr. Peters, I would be pleased if you would visit my family and me in Oxford. You could join a few friends in a hunt for raccoon or squirrels, and we could spend a night in the woods by a lake eating Brunswick stew and washing it down with lots of bourbon while we play nickel poker."

"I wouldn't miss it," I grinned.

Faulkner got out quickly and hurried into the hotel without looking back. His gray jacket was badly wrinkled, and he looked a little frail as he moved, but his back was straight with a dignity I knew I could never pull off.

Time didn't mean much anymore. I turned on the radio and was told again that a Japanese general said an invasion of California would be simple and that Pat Kelly had fought to a draw with heavyweight wrestling champ Jim Londos. While Jean Sablon sang "I Was Only Passing By," I spotted an all-night eatery I had stumbled on before. It was small, just on the fringe that turned Sunset from class to working-class, and it always had a group of guys who looked like truck drivers sitting at the counter and tables chewing coffee and settling the world's problems. I never saw any trucks on the street, so I didn't know what these guys really were or did. Maybe they were movie producers traveling incognito looking for talent. I didn't want to be discovered, so I didn't bother to flash my glowing smile when I came in and found an open red-leather stool at the counter.

"What'll it be?" said the guy behind the counter as he cleaned off a pile of crumbs in front of me. He was covered with hair, on his arms and neck, and looked as if he could hold Londos to a draw. I wondered whether Jeremy Butler had ever wrestled against Londos or Pat Kelly.

I ordered a cheese omelette, not well done, a bowl of cereal, and coffee. Three tons of fun in a corner table argued, but I couldn't get interested. The omelette was good, the cereal was crisp, and the coffee strong. I was regaining the idea that I was a functioning human being. I could have stopped at County Hospital before I went home for an X ray of my back, just in case something was cracked or broken, but without young Doc Parry there, the place held no challenge.

I got home before dawn and found a parking space right in front of the boarding house on Heliotrope. No one bothered me when I went in and up. No one was in my room when I flipped the lights on and locked the door with the little hook and latch provided by Mrs. Plaut. My one-year-old niece Lucy could have pushed through the locked door without pausing.

My suit went on a chair, and I noticed the big pile of handwritten paper on my table. It looked like a few thousand pages. Maybe it was papers I had to fill out to get an apology from the Internal Revenue Service for being harassed by them when I had no income. It turned out to be Mrs. Plaut's manuscript.

I looked at the first page of chapter fourteen on top, "What could Seymour do?" it began. "The Indian had destroyed the pianoforte and had turned on him and Sister. He dispatched the heathen with his weapon." She didn't mention what the weapon was. Maybe instead of billing Faulkner, I could send him Mrs. Plaut's manuscript and ask him for comments I could feed her, but I decided against it. A simple bill would be less cruel.

My sleep was the sleep of the self-satisfied and unemployed. In a few hours I would get up, go to my office, make out my bills, and hope there was a job lead. There were no dreams of vampire women, haunted houses, the Old South, or Cincinnati. There was just sleep.

When I woke up my watch told me it was two o'clock, but

I didn't know which two o'clock it was. The Beech-Nut clock said it was three, and the sun said it was day. Considering my line of work, it would have been reasonable to invest in a new watch. Slavick Jewelry Company on Seventh had an Elgin eighteen-jewel for $33.75. I could get twelve months to pay it off, but I knew I'd consider that a betrayal of my old man's gift.

Gunther wasn't in so I left him a note on his desk explaining that the world had been put right again with thanks to his efforts in tracking down the Culver City hideaway. Then I grabbed a coffee, stopped at a stand for a pair of chili dogs, and headed for my office.

Jeremy Butler was escorting a drunk out the front door of the Farraday Building when I arrived. The place was a mecca for the unwashed and pickled of the neighborhood. It was as if drunks could breed. Jeremy held the man gently under one arm, and the thin guy took it philosophically and quietly.

"It's over," I told Butler. "Lugosi's all right."

"Good. I've been preparing a series of poems related to vampirism," Butler said. The drunk looked interested.

"I'd like to read them when they're ready," I lied.

Jeremy nodded and took his bundle out the door.

Shelly was sitting in his single dental chair when I came in. Customerless, he was reading a dental journal.

"You know, Toby," he said, pushing his glasses back on his nose, "I can't make up my mind about who to submit the thing about vampire teeth to, a journal or *Collier's.*"

"I don't think *Collier's* would be interested," I said, moving toward my office.

"But they pay," he said reasonably. "Dental journals don't pay anything."

"I thought you were interested in prestige?" I reminded him.

Shelly shrugged, wiped his moist forehead with his soiled white jacket, and said, "Maybe I can have both."

"Maybe," I said, opening my door, "but you'll have to go with what you have on it. I don't think Sam Billings will be showing up here again. There's a good chance he'll be giving up fangs, too."

"I thought I convinced him," Shelly said, lighting a fresh cigar.

"You're very persuasive, Shel," I said, about to close myself into the windowed tomb that served as my office.

"Hey," he shouted, flipping a few pages, "you had a call."

"Who?"

"I don't know," he said. "I didn't take it. Jeremy wrote it on one of your envelopes."

Looking through my mail, I found no messages, and I didn't feel up to opening the mail. It looked like a pile of bills and no potential work. One of the bills was from Doc Hodgdon for my leg.

The task at hand was to make up my bills, but that didn't fill me with enthusiasm. Faulkner had no money, and Lugosi was just coming out of a period in which he had been on welfare. I neatly printed letters to each of them stating that my expenses had been negligible and that they owed me a fee for three days' work, since they had both given me two-day advances. Both the two-day advances were almost gone. My bill to Faulkner totaled a little over $100, and he wouldn't be paying for some time. I billed Lugosi $30. There was a good chance I'd be making the rounds in a week or two, trying to pick up subcontracts for skip tracers and fill in vacations for hotel detectives I knew.

I shoved my mail into my jacket pocket just as I heard the outside door to the dental office open. When I turned off my light and got to the door, Mrs. Lee was back in the chair.

"You remember Mrs. Lee," Shelly said to me.

Mrs. Lee's frightened eyes had trouble focusing. She clutched a knitted purse to her many bosoms like a teddy bear.

"Today we have something special prepared for our favorite patient," Shelly said in his most phony bedside manner as he patted the fat lady with his right hand and searched through the newspapers on his work stand with his left.

"Today," he continued, "we are going to do something to Mrs. Lee's bicuspids that would make the headlines tomorrow if it weren't for the war, right, Mrs. Lee?"

She moved her head in a variety of directions at the same time.

"Good afternoon, Shel," I said. "See you, Mrs. Lee."

Mrs. Lee was practicing her groaning sound when I closed the outer door and moved into the hall. My back was aching, but with an ache I recognized, which told me it would eventually go away. My knee was holding up with only a faint reminder of what had happened, and the pain in my head from Newcomb's attack in the parking lot of the Chinese restaurant was now an undetectable part of the frenetic nightmare of my cranium. I was feeling fine.

When I got to the lobby, my disposition cooled. A figure I recognized was going over the listings in the lobby, which was tough since the lights were out and he had to use the trickle of sun filtering in from outside.

"I'll save you the trouble," I said. Cawelti the cop looked at me, and we both listened to my footsteps echo on the tile.

He stepped back with his hands in his coat pocket and a smirk on his face. He was trying to erase the humiliation I had witnessed when Phil almost strangled him. I could read it on his face. He could have taken some pointers from Faulkner and Lugosi on how to accept humiliation, but I had the feeling he wouldn't accept advice from me.

I walked right up to him, violating his space as much as I could without having to actually smell his hair tonic.

"We going to have a shootout in the hall?" I said.

He snickered, maybe on the verge of breaking.

"No one gets away with what you did to me, Peters," he said through closed teeth. "Brother or no brother, I'm going to be on your back. You made yourself a bad enemy."

"Are there good ones?" I asked.

"Some time. Some place," he said, touching my chest with his finger, "you're going to have to even up with me."

"Look," I said, pulling out my notebook, "just give me your name and address and I'll put you on my mailing list. All my enemies are on it. I have a newsletter with the latest information about my injuries, personal life, the works."

He knocked the notebook out of my hand, and I threw a right into his stomach as hard as I could. I could have delivered a harder blow if I were a foot farther back, but it did just fine. He went against the lobby wall.

I thought he might go for his gun, but he came up with a mad smile.

"Assaulting an officer," he gasped.

I looked into a dark corner for my notebook and saw it coming at me in the hand of Jeremy Butler.

"No one hit you," Butler said to Cawelti. "I've been standing there cleaning up. You fell."

Cawelti faced us, his eyes darting from one to the other. "I . . ." he started, and then without another word he turned and went through the door.

"He has the persona of a victim," Butler said, his hands on his massive hips, "and the ego of a spoiled child. A poor psychological combination."

"He's a cop," I explained.

Butler nodded, turned, and disappeared into the gray of the building to continue his attack on decay and dirt. I, in turn, went out into the late afternoon, saw no Cawelti, and drove to Griffith Park to watch a couple of sailors who looked like they were twelve feeding a camel peanuts. For part of a second I considered the possibility of lining up behind Tony Zale, Hank

Greenberg, and Tony Martin and joining the Army or Navy, but I was too old and too torn up and the feeling passed.

I found a theater in Hollywood that had *The Maltese Falcon,* which I had seen three times. I sat through it a fourth time, which made me feel better. By the time I got out, it was almost dark. I headed home to get some rest before I had to pick up Carmen.

Parking was bad. Someone was blaring a radio, and people were laughing. It was a party and I wasn't invited. When I found a place in the alley where I stood a fifty-fifty chance of getting a ticket, I looked up at Mrs. Plaut's boarding house. The light in my room was on. It could have been Gunther waiting for me over a cup of tea or Mrs. Plaut anxious for my literary comments on her massive tome. It could have been Cawelti bent on vengeance or my former wife Anne ready to give up her life of sanity. But it was none of the above. I leaned against my speckled fender and looked up at the window. A figure passed in front and out of sight and then it returned. It paused in the window, looking down. Our eyes met. It was Bedelia Sue Frye in her vampire character.

I considered the possibilities and options, weighed the rewards and pain, and waved up at her before climbing back into the car. She watched as I pulled out and drove away. I can take a lot of punishment, but the dark side of Bedelia Sue Frye was a consummation I could do without.

It wouldn't be the first time I had spent a night in Shelly's dental chair. It probably wouldn't be the last either. If I could crank it back past the rusty point, it would go almost horizontal. Of course there was always the chance Carmen would let me stay with her, but it had never happened, and I didn't expect it. I took off my jacket, brushed my teeth with the spare frayed brush in my drawer, and shaved, deciding to deal with the daytime Bedelia the next day.

The envelopes of junk mail tumbled from my pocket, and

I picked them up. The flap on one of them came open, and I could see a handwritten note on it in Jeremy's fine hand. I scratched my smooth face, let out a yawn loud enough to shake Hoover Avenue, and read the message. There was a phone number and the following:

"Call Gary Cooper. Urgent."

I tucked the envelope back in my jacket, crawled into the dental chair, adjusted my back so I wouldn't lie on the sore spot, and fell asleep to the lullaby of traffic, battles, and dead dreams that floated up from Hoover Street, penetrated the walls, and surrounded me with a familiar blanket.

THE END